THEFT OF A NATION

by
William W. Baker

Defender's Publications
P.O. Box 11134
Las Vegas, NV 89111

ISBN 0-910643-00-8

2nd Printing - 1984

COVER:
The cover is reproduced from a painting completed in 1973 by Sliman Mansur, a Palestinian born and educqted in the West Bank. It portrays an elderly Arab porter carrying grain through the streets of the Old City of Jerusalem. The fraying rope indicates the deterioration of hope that the current Israeli state will permit the Palestinian People their rightful pursuit of autonomy and self-determination. The old porter has the strength and determination to carry his beloved city, represented by the golden Dome of the Rock of Mohammed and Abraham, to a position of respect and honor. The bulging sack represents the continued oppression and varied attempts of the Jewish state to discourage the Palestinian People from carrying their city to independence. The size of the burden and fraying rope are reminders that the burden cannot be put down until there is sovereign recognition for the Palestinian servant. Like all Palestinians, the old man is determined to carry his beloved Jerusalem as a faithful servant, but never as a slave.

DEDICATION

Dedicated to my dear daughters Julie and Tricia, in the hope that their generation will witness the return and restoration of the Palestinian Nation to its former state of indigenous autonomy, and a truly lasting peace between Arab and Jew will once and for all prevail.

CONTENTS

"TO THE JEW AS A MAN—EVERYTHING: TO JEWS AS A NATION—NOTHING."

—*Count Stanislas Clermont-Tonnerre*
to the French Assembly, Oct. 12, 1789

"PEACE IN PALESTINE CANNOT BE ACHIEVED BY FORCE, BUT ONLY THROUGH UNDERSTANDING."

—*Albert Einstein*

"THE FAULT, DEAR BRUTUS, IS NOT IN OUR STARS, BUT IN OURSELVES, THAT WE ARE UNDERLINGS."

—*William Shakespeare*

"Thus says the Lord of hosts, the God of Israel, "Amend your ways and your deeds, and I will let you dwell in this place. Do not trust in deceptive words, saying, 'This is the temple of the Lord, the temple of the Lord, the temple of the Lord.' "For if you truly amend your ways and your deeds, if you truly practice justice between a man and his neighbor, if you do not oppress the alien, the orphan, or the widow, and you do not shed innocent blood in this place, nor walk after other gods to your own ruin, then I will let you dwell in this place, in the land I gave to your fathers forever and ever. Behold, you are trusting deceptive words to no avail. Will you steal, murder, and commit adultery, and swear falsely, and offer sacrifices to Baal, and walk after other gods that you have not known, then come and stand before Me in this house, which is called by My name, and say, 'We are delivered!'—that you may do all these abominations? "Has this house which is called by My name, become a den of robbers in your sight? Behold, I, even I, have seen it," declares the Lord."

Jeremiah 7:3-11

PREFACE

Palestine. . . . . a land of contrast, chaos and conflict; center of a world-shattering, nation-dividing dichotomy; a land with a legacy of bombs, bullets and death!

Palestine. . . . . where entire cultures and nationalities have been dispersed and displaced; home of factionalized fanaticism, firebrand rhetoric, and the waging of a colossal propaganda war unparalleled within the confines of world history.

Palestine. . . . . where historical brothers wage a relentless war spanning the boundaries of historical humanity, encompassing the twentieth century, still without solution or conciliation.

Countless books and publications have attempted to define and depict the conflict, but few have presented the total picture of the historical background of both the land and the contestants. Fewer still have dared present reasonable and equitable suggestions for a lasting solution to the Palestinian dispute. Indeed, many publications have succeeded in merely exacerbating the conflict by the expression of the author's personal bias or prejudice given in support of his treatise. Jewish authors lay claim to a biblical promise to support the continued occupation of Arab lands and the ongoing expansionism instigated by each succeeding Israeli government.

Militant Palestinian authors threaten total annihilation of Israel unless their land is returned to them. Radical Arab leaders vow to "drive the Jews into the sea" as punishment for the seizure of their country.

Major religious authors representative of a large segment of evangelicalism claim the bible fully supports the concept of a "Jewish Homeland" and, therefore, evangelicals should be supportive of the expulsion of the Palestinian people from their native country. This teaching has become one of the primary contributing factors to the middle east conflict and partly responsible for the continued proliferation and substantiation of a distorted and faulty interpretation of biblical prophecy.

An oil-dependent world lies divided in support of the principle participants of the conflict, Arabs and Jews, Israelis and Palestinians. The single most explosive situation faced by America's President and Congress is the real possibility of a mideast war which would contain the potential of escalation to worldwide proportions. Both Arab and Jew possess the capability of nuclear warfare and have demonstrated little restraint or reservation to employ such devastation if either party should conclude it to be necessary for national survival.

Our present day world stands on the brink of global disaster with the ever-growing possibility of a direct confrontation between the two super powers. When and if this confrontation should occur will in part be determined by the events which occur in the middle east drama.

One purpose of this book is to present an objective and impartial view of both the contested land and the contestants. We will examine such pertinent questions as: who were the original Semites? Who really was the first to occupy the land known historically as Palestine? Where did the Arabs and the Jews originally come from? How, when and by whom was the land first divided?

Another purpose of this book will be to carefully examine the political involvements and ramifications for America and the world. Basic political questions such as: should the United States maintain a policy of unswerving support for the Israeli government despite America's increasing need for allies among the emerging nations of the world? And what of the growing dependence of America upon the third world Arab countries for important oil and fuel supplies? What treaties exist between Israel and the United States? Is America bound to support Israeli occupation of Palestine with military intervention of our own armed forces?

Of special importance will be the consideration of the political history of Palestine from its ancient status in secular and biblical history to its present-day stronghold of Zionism. What role did western European powers play in creating the current crisis? What about the Balfour Declaration and the United Nations Partition of 1948? These and many other questions must be explored and understood before an equitable conclusion can be made.

A primary goal of this book is to present a thorough examination of the biblical passages often cited as "proof texts" in support of a "Jewish Homeland." Each important text will be examined by use and application of the hermeneutical rules of interpretation which apply to every work of literature, including the Bible. Each "prophecy" long assumed to corroborate the Jewish occupation of Palestine will be examined in light of the original language in which it was written. A careful consideration of past historical events and the latest archaeological findings will be presented in an effort to establish as fact that many biblical prophecies have been fulfilled and must not be paralleled with contemporary events or cultural changes of the twentieth century.

Did God promise all those claiming to be Jews of every age and every land and nation a special homeland? Did He fulfill His own Covenant with Abraham? Does God support and desire dishonesty, distortion and deceit? Determinative answers to all of these questions are crucial to the formulation of an honest and objective understanding of the mideast crisis, and will prove influential in affecting one's understanding of the Biblical passages which lie at the very heart of the Jewish and Palestinian conflict.

This book is written with the hope that once enlightened, citizens of every country and culture will weigh equitably the many factors comprising the Palestinian issue, and only then will voice their support of a just resolution for all parties.

This author believes that all conflict everywhere and throughout the annals of human history has been caused primarily by injustice, ignorance and deceit. True justice, and consequently true peace, depends upon the emergence and assimilation of truth, impartiality, and the sincere desire to right all wrongs once those wrongs are exposed. Truth is never expendable and must remain the determinative force for change and a truly lasting peace.

There will be no peace or solutions forthcoming while those who boast of freedom and democracy are intolerant of the views and culture of others living in their own land. There can be no peace while political powers forbid the practice of freedom of speech. There will be no peace while men malign one another and distort truth to win an election to public office, or while politicians conspire to enslave and imprison those who oppose or disagree with them; while men profess to be "righteous" yet deny the basic liberty of free thought and expression; while men prate of morals and idealism, yet sell their souls amid the hypocrisies of the hour and that which is expedient or popular; while men claim truth to be solely theirs alone, maintaining they "have a right" to disinherit, to destroy another race or culture of men, THERE WILL BE NO PEACE!

Chapter 1

THE CONTESTANTS

IN THIS CHAPTER we will define the principal parties involved in the current struggle of the middle east drama. We will consider the past and present status of the Semites, Hebrews (Jews), Arabs, and Palestinian People (Arabs).

We begin with a brief historical examination of the origination and background of each principal in an effort to answer the important question of who was the first to live in Palestine, and where and when did the current inhabitants enter the land.

THE SEMITES

The word "Semite" or "semitical" does not occur in the biblical text. The term was derived from the name of Noah's oldest son, Shem. Semite was a term used to identify those people whose ancestors once spoke any one of a group of languages which, with the decipherment of the cuneiform writing in the 19th century, were found to be cognates. The languages are Assyro-Babylonian, Hebrew, Aramaic, Arabic, and Ethiopic. The people whose ancestors once spoke them are the Assyrians, Babylonians, Chaldeans, Amorites, Aramaens, Canaanites (including Phoenicians), Hebrews, Arabians, and Abyssinians. Most of the Semites of today now speak Arabic, which is also spoken by millions of non-Semites. Ethiopic is spoken in Ethiopia, and hebrew primarily by Jews now living in Israel, though Jews and others study the language elsewhere.

Archaeology has confirmed that the ancestors of the aforementioned people demonstrate strong similarities in language, religion, social institutions, even physical features. Thus the conclusion that these ancestors must have lived at one time in the ancient past as one people in the same locale. The majority of scholarly opinion now favors the argument that the original home of the Semites was the Arabian peninsula. (See Bibliography and suggested reading list.)

It is generally agreed that the Semites in 3500 B.C. overran in successive movements every part of the Fertile Crescent. Two major Semitic migrations took place: One followed the route along the eastern coast of the Arabian peninsula and struck root in the Tigro-Euphrates valley, already populated by the highly civilized Sumerians, who were non-Semites. Because of their relatively larger number, the Semites dominated and their spoken language prevailed; but they had to learn writing and numerous other intelligent activities. The resulting mixture of the two groups is considered to be Semitic and this union produced the Assyrians, Babylonians and Chaldeans of both secular and biblical history. The second migration followed the route along the western coast, and eventually planted itself in the midst of the earliest Hamitic population of Egypt. The number of Semites being relatively small, the mixture remained Hamitic, producing the Egyptians and the Pharoahs who preserved their own language. A third migration around 2600 B.C. brought the Amorites into the fertile crescent; these included the Canaanites, who occupied what is now Palestine, and also Lebanon. Those who occupied Lebanon were known to the Greeks as Phoenicians. Between the years 1500 and 1200 B.C. the Aramaens made their way to what is now Syria. Please note that the land called "Palestine" was occupied long before the emergence of any nation or group called "Hebrews." The name Palestine is the oldest name of the country, and is called 'pelesheth' in the Hebrew, and 'phylistieim' in the Greek. Both refer to the original inhabitants of the land, the Philistines, hence the name of the land was called Palestine, meaning "the land of the Philistines."

But where then did the name "Israel" come from, and when was this name applied to Palestine? "Israel" is a hebrew word (Yisra'el), which means, "He strives with God (and prevails)." The term is used biblically to designate both the son of Isaac who was called Jacob, and his (Jacob's) descendants, the twelve tribes of the Hebrews. (See Genesis 32:28; 35:10) Archaeology and world history reveal that the Hebrews invaded occupied Palestine in 1400 B.C. It was then that the term "Israel" was first applied to the land.

THE HEBREWS

Apart from the biblical teaching that the descendants of Jacob were known as Israelites, very little is known as to the origin of the Hebrews. Many of their early descendants interchanged the terms "Israel" and "Jews." But we are without historical and biblical evidence as to the origin of "Hebrews." It is safe to say the majority of historical and biblical scholars currently contend that the Hebrews were really the "Habiru," "Khapiru" or "Apiru," all names for a people who were not an ethnic group, but who formed a class of society in various geographic areas. This society had no social status and owned no land. The Hapiru or Hebrews originally did not comprise a nation or nationality, but were wandering people greatly restricted as regards financial means and were without citizenship and social status.

They worked as merchants, mercenaries, voluntary serfs and even slaves. Ancient records show the "Habiru" to be scattered over Western Asia for centuries until 1100 B.C. Mostly Semitic, they are mentioned in the famous Tell-el-Amarna Tablets as making war upon the Canaanite towns and population who were Semites. They also battled the Philistines who had entered the country from the Aegean Islands. The Philistines were fierce warriors and eventually gave their name to the land. (See Suggested Reading list for further study.)

Those who inhabited the land of Palestine after 1400 B.C. called themselves "Jews," Yehudi in the Hebrew, denoting one who belonged to the tribe of Judah or one of the two tribes of the Southern Kingdom. The word Jew does not even appear in the Old Testament until the time of the prophet Jeremiah in 626 B.C.

Etymologically, it has been debated whether "Hebrew" is to be traced to Eber, the father of Peleg and Koktan (Genesis 10:24,25; 11:12-16) or is derived from the Hebrew root meaning "to pass over" which would have been the case for the Habiru crossing from the Euphrates into Palestine. Accordingly then, our conclusion is that the ancestors of the Jews and Israelites of 1400 B.C. were indeed the "Habirus" from which the name "Hebrew" is most probably extracted. The state or states established by the Israelites were destroyed by the great Assyrian and Babylonian empires in 700 B.C. and 550 B.C., respectively.

THE ARABS

The word "Arab," in the Hebrew "arav," means desert or inhabitant of the desert. The first time the name Arabian is mentioned among historical records occurs in an inscription of Shalmanaser III of Assyria which commemorates his victory over the Aramean king of Damascus and his allies Ahab, King of Israel and Jundub, the Arabian chief. The encounter took place at Karkar, north of Hamah (Syria) in 854 B.C. The camel is also mentioned for the first time in this inscription. The word "Arab" or "Arabian" appears in the biblical text in several locations including Joshua 15:52, Isaiah 21:13, Acts 2:11 and Galatians 1:17.

After the previously mentioned Semitic migrations occurred, no further appreciable migrations took place. Meanwhile, the Semitic tribes who remained within the peninsula became known as Arabians, and their languages developed into major Arabic dialects, one in the north of the peninsula and the other in the south. The southern Arabs claim descendancy from an ancestor called Kahtan, son of 'Abir,' son of Shalikh, son of Arfakhshad, son of Shem, son of Noah. Kahtan is undoubtedly the Biblical "joktan" of Genesis 10:26, and the names of his descendants reappear as Arab place names. The northern tribes are descendants of Ishmael and retained the distinctive name of "Ishmaelites."

All the geographic areas to which the Semites had migrated became the object of successive conquests by foreign powers, more notably Persia under Cyrus, Macedonia under Phillip II, father of Alexander, and finally under Alexander himself. A final conquest by the Romans proved to be the longest and most devastating.

Throughout all these many conquests the people were subjected to foreign rule but not to deportation or exile, save for the Hebrew element of the Semitic tribes, whose deportation and exile comprises the subject matter of the major and minor prophetic books of the Bible.

In the year 370 A.D. the Roman government under Constantine accepted Christianity as the official religion of the Roman Empire. Many living in the occupied areas were converted to the state religion of Christianity, but others maintained their Christian faith from the time of Christ and the first century Church. In 635 A.D. a new and large scale Semitic migration took place under the banner of Islam. This was in fact an Arab-Moslem invasion, which drove the Romans out of North Africa, Egypt, Mesopatamia, Syria, Palestine and Lebanon.

It did not deport the inhabitants, but did impress upon them the Arabic language. Moreover, with the exception of most of those who were already either Jews or Christians, the rest of the population accepted the Moslem faith. The invasion conquered other territories also in the East and in the West. But from this brief historical outline we can account for the original Arab people.

THE PALESTINIAN ARABS

One must realize that the ancestors of the great majority of the Arabs of Palestine did not enter Palestine with the Moslem invasion. In fact, Palestinians are primarily descendants of those Semites who occupied Palestine from time immemorial, namely, the Canaanites and other Semitic tribes, and of the Jews who were taken into captivity by the Assyrians or the Babylonians, and ultimately absorbed by the remainder of the population. Naturally, they also include the descendants of those non-Semites who may have remained behind after the Persians, Macedonians, Romans and other conquerors had been driven out by the Arab invasion, and who were completely Arabised by that invasion. This applies to the remnants of subsequent invaders including the Crusaders.

The Ottoman Moslem rule which lasted for 400 years and which came to an end in 1917, did not in any way alter the Arabic or Moslem structure of the people of Palestine. The small Jewish and Christian minorities who likewise had been Arabised, continued to live in peace with the Moslems. Though both were minorities, they were accepted as friends and neighbors in good standing.

HISTORICAL CONCLUSION

From a cursory examination of ancient Palestinian history, it becomes apparent that the ancestors of the Palestine Arabs of today were indeed living in Palestine at the same time as the ancestors of the Semitic Jews.The Biblical record affirms that the Arabs and Jews were first cousins, being descendants of one common ancestor, Abraham, by his three wives Sarah, Hagar, and Ketura.

As will be seen in the following chapters, the present-day Jews now occupying Palestine are but mere fragments and in no way traceable to the former Hebrews or Habiru who once conquered the land of Canaan. Semitical people existed long before they were joined by these same Habirus thus discrediting the commonly accepted notion that only modern day Jews are "semitical."

Those Palestine Arabs still living in Palestine are true descendants of the original semitical inhabitants. Their roots do not lie in Syria or Lebanon, Jordan or Egypt, but rather the only country they have ever known as their homeland, the land of Palestine.

CURRENT STATUS OF THE CONTESTANTS

Persons interested in a just and lasting peace in the Middle East should be aware of the basic events which precipitated the present conflict which includes the detailed arguments and major points of view of both parties. We wish to concern ourselves with the facts and historical events which set the stage for the current drama. How did the current situation come about? How did the Jews come to be the governing power in Palestine? We will attempt to present a brief summary of the vital events relevant to these questions in chronological order.

(1) For an extended time in history the Jews living in most of the Christian countries of Western Europe were discriminated against, resulting in harassment and persecution. The persecution was often accompanied by cruel violence to life and property. This collective discrimination resulted in real injustice to the Jews. This injustice strengthened the resolve in the hearts of many Jews to realize a long cherished desire to re-establish a Jewish state which would house all Jews; a state which would save them from any further persecution and harassment.

This desire was strongest quite expectedly, in those countries responsible for the more grievous persecution. But the only country which was acceptable to the majority of persecuted Jews was the country where the Jews had once upon a time (over 2000 years ago) established a state for a relatively short period of historical time. This same "state" eventually broke up into two small and separate states.

This desire to re-establish a state and escape persecution gave rise to the formation in 1897 of the Zionist Organization. This organization was charged with the task of achieving the desired goal of a Jewish state. It is important to note at this juncture that those Jews being persecuted had no ethnic connection with the semitic Jews who had once lived and occupied a portion of Palestine. Remember that the original semitic Jews were carried away into slavery and dispersion on several historical occasions by various Kings and Kingdoms to which we will devote a portion of our study.

Assyria first made contact with the Northern Kingdom of Israel when Shalmaneser II routed the combined forces of Damascus, Hamath, Israel and other states in the battle of Karkar in 854 B.C. Under Tiglath-pileser III, one of the outstanding monarchs of antiquity, Assyria captured Samaria in 735 B.C. His successor, the great King Sargon, quelled an uprising at Samaria (Northern Israel) in 722 B.C. and after a three year siege he conquered the city once again and deported the inhabitants to Assyria, except for the very poor who remained behind. Sargon's grandson, Esarhaddon, and his great-grandson Ashur-banipal, imported to the region of Samaria some conquered peoples from the East who intermarried with those Jews remaining behind in Samaria. Their offspring became known as Samaritans. One may verify this account in secular history as well as biblical accounts. (See suggested reading list at close of book.) Biblical passages relating this story include II Kings 17:6,7; 18:11, 12; Ezra 4:2,10 and II Kings 25:12. The Northern Kingdom was comprised of the Ten Tribes of the Israelite nation, and many were absorbed by the peoples among whom they had previously settled.

By 625 B.C. Assyria's power was on the wane, and a new super-power moved into prominence. The Babylonians, under their King Nebuchadnezzar who reigned from 604-562 B.C., conquered the Southern Kingdom of Israel in 604 B.C. The king removed the ceremonial vessels used in the temple services, and along with the nobility of Judah, returned them to Babylon. The Israelite King Jehoiachin, along with his mother, his wives, 3000 princes, 7000 men of might, and 1000 artisans, were all brought to Babylon in the year 595 B.C. (See II Chronicles 36:2-6, II Kings 24:14-16.) Eleven years later (586 B.C) Nebuchadnezzar burned the temple and destroyed the city of Jerusalem, deporting into Babylon all but the poorest. (II Kings 25:2-21) These dispersions are called today the "Diaspora," referring to those Jews carried off into captivity during both historical conquests.

There were other captivities of a smaller scale carried out by the rulers of Egypt and Syria, and Rome under Pompey. These too helped further scatter the Israelites. In all historical truth, those Jews who once occupied Palestine or "the promised land" of the Bible, were once and for all scattered and diffused among the peoples of the world.

From the time of Alexander the Great (332 B.C.) the Israelites emigrated by the thousands into the neighboring countries and cities for purposes of trade and commerce. By the time of Jesus Christ the diaspora was several times the population of Palestine. Archaeology confirms a temple of Jehovah existed in the Egyptian city of Elephantine in 525 B.C., a result of the dispersion and captivities we have just related.

Those Jews in 1897 who desired to once again possess Palestine as their homeland were in no way connected with the semitic Jews of some 2500 years previous. This is attributable to the admixture of blood through marriage; but it is also due to the large number of non-semites who were converted to Judaism. Perhaps the classic example of this occurrence is the Khazzar tribe living in present day Russia. Their wholesale conversion took place in the 8th century A.D., and many of the present Russian Jews are descendants of this tribe.

(2) In 1917 during World War I, the British government gave a promise to the Zionists that they (the British) would fully support their aims and goals with regard to Palestine. Their promise was embodied in the famous Balfour Declaration. In 1916 the Arab population revolted against France and Britain after discovering the extraordinary deceit practiced by both major powers in planning the conquest of their native homeland, and the eventual handing-over of their country to the Zionist Organization. As one reads and ponders the plans and attitudes of the major European powers towards the Arab people of Palestine, one is hard pressed to find a comparable story of blatant deceit and dishonor among historical or fictional literature.

While the British accepted the aid of the Arab people in fighting the German invasion of the Middle East, they secretly conspired to "sell out" their Arab allies to the Zionist dream of a new homeland. The British Secretary General sent a letter to the Zionist Organization and specifically to Baron Rothschild, encouraging the Jews to "take" Palestine as their homeland.

Although the Balfour document was completed as early as 1915, it was kept secret by the British in order to enjoy the aid of the Arab people in fighting the Germans. We now know it was kept secret also because a serious division was already in place among the orthodox Jews and those adhering to the Zionist Organization's claims and manifesto. (See my recommended reading on this topic in the list of suggested readings at the close of the book.)

The Balfour Declaration took two years to write, yet contains a mere 67 words. The wording came from the British Foreign Office, but the text had been revised in the Zionist offices of America and England. So it was on November 2, 1917, when General Allenby was pushing up through Palestine with his British Army, that Arthur James Balfour, the British Foreign Secretary, issued the famous declaration bearing his name. This document gave official British approval of Palestine as a national home for the Jewish people. The text of the Declaration reads as follows:

> *"His Majesty's Government views with favor the establishment in Palestine of a national home for the Jewish people and will use their best endeavors to facilitate the achievement of this object, it being clearly understood that nothing shall be done which may prejudice the civil and religious rights of non-Jewish communities in Palestine, or the rights and political status enjoyed by Jews in any other country."*

The British ruled Palestine for the next 30 years under a so-called "mandate" issued by the old League of Nations. And it was at this point in time that the Arab nationals began resisting the British occupation of their homeland. The Balfour Declaration gave the Zionists the backing of a major Middle East power, thus Zionism, both Religious and Political Zionism, was launched under this mandate.

History reveals the British were to experience the wrath of the Jew as well as the Arab during the next thirty years of rioting, terrorism, murder and untold atrocities. For the first time a new term was used with absolutely no meaning, the term "National Home" for the Zionist Jews.

By 1914 only 3000 Jewish farmers lived in Palestine. At the close of the first World War (1918) the population of Palestine was divided into 644,000 Arabs and only 56,000 Jews. Obviously the Jews had never held the land of Palestine either numerically or industrially in the past 2500 years! This land had belonged to the semitic ancestors of the modern-day Arab People. To demonstrate that both the British and the

Jews knew this to be true, we must note once again the third clause of the Balfour Declaration,

> *"it being clearly understood that nothing shall be done which may prejudice the civil and religious rights of non-Jewish communities in Palestine, or the rights and political status enjoyed by Jews in any other country."*

This statement ranks among the most infamous ever penned as to double talk, subtle deceit and subterfuge. This third clause was added, supposedly, *to protect the native, majority population of Arabs* residing in Palestine. Read it again! Now consider what has taken place from 1917 to the present day. The entire country of Palestine has been "taken" by political Zionists, and it would seem the entire world has believed, supported and participated in the "theft" of an entire country from an entire nation! Lands, homes, customs, economy, everything which formerly belonged to the Arab people have been replaced with Israeli control and influence, including the very name of the country! The assumption that Palestine is the Jewish homeland and they only require aid to get back what is "rightfully" theirs has been so well propagandized that one is accused of "discrimination" or anti-semitism if not supportive of the occupation and theft of Palestine. But we must insist on presenting the facts regardless of the emotional response incurred from others, or there will never be a just and lasting settlement of this tragic injustice.

According to the Balfour Declaration, General Allenby and James Balfour promised the native Arabs of Palestine that their rights would be respected. Likewise, so did the San Remo Conference and President Woodrow Wilson in the twelfth of his Fourteen Points. Yes, all have "promised" equitable treatment to the Arab people, yet explicitly supporting and even financing the complete destruction and displacement of the Arab people. Somehow, the rights of the original Semites, who had never left their homes, their lands or their country, their rights have been ignored as if they are undeserving of such rights to liberty, self-determination, personal ambition and aspiration, and freedom of choice.

The United States and France supported the Balfour Declaration not from a sense of justice or compassion for the plight of the Jews, but rather from purely military and political considerations. The religious and non-sophisticated citizens of the three countries (Britain, France and United States) accepted the mandate blindly, primarily because they thought it somehow fulfilled certain biblical promises to the Jews. Other citizens in those same countries supported the Declaration as a legitimate method for redressing the injustices inflicted upon an innocent people, the Jews.

But herein lies the heart of the problem, and an unparalleled example of supra-hypocritical, consistently inconsistent contradiction! It seems that none of the politicians or citizens who were so enthusiastically supportive of the mandate had realized that the method they were using to redress an injustice to the Jews involved the infliction of an EVEN GREATER INJUSTICE on innocent people! They totally ignored the accepted ethical principle that two wrongs do not make a right. The injustice was further aggravated by the fact that all participants seemed oblivious to the fact that the persons on the receiving end of this new injustice, namely the Palestinians, had never been a party to the persecution of the Jews! So it is that the persecuted became the persecutor. Those who would decry the discrimination and ridicule of a biased and prejudiced Europe began their own assault upon an absolutely innocent and gentle people.

I have yet to discover any book of history which asks the important question, who gave the three world powers, including the Zionist Organization, the right to "give away" and to take control of the Palestinian people and their country? Nor have I read in any of the thousands of books and journals written about the Jews and Arabs and the Land, a satisfactory answer to that question.

I call your attention a final time to the third clause of the Declaration or mandate. The wording is carefully prepared to avoid even the naming of, much less validating the existence of, the Arab people. They were simply called the "non-Jewish community," as if *THEY* were the actual minority in the land, instead of the immigrating Jews who comprised a mere 8% of the total population.

Sadly, little has changed from that day to this, for the

displaced, dispersed and even despised Palestinian People are ignored by all as if they simply do not exist.

(3) It is a little known fact, nevertheless a true statement, that prior to the Balfour Fiasco, those few Jews living in and among the Arab people of Palestine were living in peace and understanding. As an archaeologist who has lived among both Arab and Jew, I can refer the reader to a most conspicuous example of the former trust and peaceful relationship which once existed. A weak minority group, even shunned by fellow Jews, is the Smaritan people residing in Nablus. Though a minority, and though they are very close relatives to the Jews (see "Contestants", Part I) they were accorded mutual respect and acceptance by the Palestinian people. This glaring reversal of attitude and action by those Jews who "took" Palestine from the Arab people has understandably increased the bitterness in the hearts of the Palestinians. Again, the various actions and attitudes taken to redress an old injustice by the perpetration of a new and irrelevant injustice, constitutes the Palestinian Problem of Today.

As you progress through the rest of this book you will have cause to remember this chapter, for in it are contained the reasons for the crisis today. These two major elements compose the crisis:

(a) An attempt by certain forces to halt, redress or remove the injustice inflicted on the Palestinians, and

(b) A counter attempt by other forces or nations to perpetuate the injustice and even to expand it.

Any sincere deliberation, whether undertaken by nations, statesmen, or the ordinary citizen, must first come to grips with these two elements. The day and time for empty rhetoric, pious platitudes and political aggrandizement is over! A violent, ever chaotic world of divided nations demands an answer. What will that answer be?

Chapter 2

IMMIGRATION AND THE UNITED NATIONS

AS INCREASING NUMBERS of foreign Jews began immigrating to Palestine at the close of World War I, they were opposed, as would be expected, by the Palestinian inhabitants. Slowly, the newcomers extended their grasp of land ownership by rather dubious methods. It is a matter of public record that a Zionist owned bank, the Anglo-Palestine Bank, would lend money to Arab citizens who were hard pressed by the ravages of war and crop failure. The money was loaned at exorbitant rates of interest, and when payment could not be made, land was seized and became "payment" for the loan. Full scale expropriation followed which included every conceivable entity, from sheep herds to glass manufacturing companies; from import companies to school systems. Thus, the battle lines were drawn, and the ferocious bloodletting began in earnest, and for the next thirty years hatred and distrust was manifest between the Arab and the Jew.

Long before there was a Palestine Liberation Organization (PLO) there was the Irgun, a zealous terrorist organization of Zionists who were unflinching in their dedication to the violent elimination of any opponent whether Arab, British, or Jew. The one time notorious leader of this underground guerilla group was no less a personage than Menachem Begin, Prime Minister of Israel. Among the more infamous terrorist acts remembered by the world, was the bombing of the King David Hotel in East Jerusalem on July 22, 1946. This bombing killed nearly one hundred innocent people, many of them Jews as well as Arabs. Numerous wire service reports credited Begin as the original planner and instigator of that bombing. This point is noteworthy in that Mr. Begin has constantly spoken of the Palestinian People as "terrorists," and perhaps we should accept his evaluation based upon his own unique qualifications which enable him to recognize and relate to terrorists on a personal level. A detailed study of both the Irgun and PLO and other terrorist groups of both sides will be considered in Chapter 5. My point is, that radical terrorist organizations and acts were not conceived and first implemented by the Arab people.

On May 14, 1948, the present-day "State of Israel" was born from the passage in the United Nations, which was formerly the old League of Nations, of the Partition of Palestine. Once again the various nations of the world took the liberty to determine that the European Jews who had immigrated to Palestine should be given half the land in order to settle the fierce struggle between the newly arriving Jews and the Arab defenders. Once again the impetus for the Zionist dream of their own homeland was reinforced.

During the British occupation of Palestine in 1918, the population consisted of 644,000 Palestinian Arabs, and 56,000 Jews. Other small ethnic groups existed but they were insignificantly small and they need not complicate our figures. The Jews formed a mere 8% of the total population.

When the British left in 1948, the population consisted of 1,350,000 Palestine Arabs and 650,000 Jews. The Jewish ratio increased from 8 to 32½%. Notice the increase of the Palestinians during the thirty-one years of the mandate was very little more than double. This was to be expected as a result of natural increases. The Jewish population, however, increased during the same period by more than eleven times! This phenomenal increase was not "miraculous" or "supernatural" as even some misguided ministers and teachers have proposed, but rather attributable to the Jewish immigration which continued to flow into the country in great numbers, all the while against the wishes of the original, majority population.

By the end of the mandate the Jews had acquired approximately an area of 580 square miles out of a total land area of Palestine of 101,635 miles. In other words, at the end of the mandate the Jews owned about 5.7% of the total land of the country. The 1948 U.N. Partition gave the Jews sovereignty over 56% of the total area of Palestine. That is nearly *ten times as much land as they had* legally and actually owned! Just as dramatically, the partition placed an equal number of Palestinian Arabs under the domination of the Jews. According to the partition scheme, the Jewish "state" contained some 498,000 Jews and 497,000 Palestinian Arabs. But the vast majority of these Arab people were now found to be living on "Jewish land," given to the Jews by the United Nations. This was the very motivation needed to provoke the Jews to do everything possible to force the Arabs to flee their homes and country, and to become refugees for the first time in their history.

It is clear then that the Palestinian refugees of today are not the result of their own "free choice" to leave their inheritance and homeland, willfully becoming refugees rather than remain citizens of Palestine. This is a part of the popular propaganda campaign advanced by the Zionist politicians. It is utterly amazing that any rational human being would begin to believe such a ridiculous statement, yet the wide acceptance of this ploy reveals the extent of ignorance on behalf of many, as to the true facts and occurrences surrounding the Middle East Crisis.

If you will recall that before the U.N. Partition, the Jews only owned 580 square miles, and the rest was owned legally, and for centuries, by Palestinian Arabs either individually or collectively in the form of communal lands or state domains. This being the true status back in 1948, is it any wonder why the Palestinians flatly rejected the Partition?

In the ensuing struggle the Jews were able to occupy still more territory by means of force. By the time of the armistice of 1948 the Jews were *in possession of 78% of the total area of the country!* Even more than was proposed by the Partition of the U.N. This occupied land included all buildings, furniture, industrial plants, orchards and groves, and all that the refugees left behind. The result was that out of nearly one million Arabs, only 160,000 remained in the new Jewish state; 500,000 stayed in the Gaza Strip held by Egypt, and on the West Bank of the Jordan River, taken over by Jordan. At least 800,000 Palestinians were dispersed as refugees; most ended up in one of the 54 refugee camps in Israel, Jordan, Syria and Lebanon, where they remained virtually forgotten by the world. By 1967 the refugees had increased to about 1,344,000.

On June 5, 1967, the "six day war" occurred, and the whole of Palestine was then occupied, and the ranks of the refugees driven from their homeland grew to 1,500,000. None of the refugees who were displaced in 1948 or subsequent years including 1967, have been permitted to return to their lands or properties.

For this reason the United Nations Commission on Human Rights drafted, on March 23, 1972, a resolution which not only deplored the militaristic expansionism of the Jewish government in acquiring Arab land and possessions, but also called upon the Jews to "permit all persons who have fled the occupied territories or who have been deported or expelled therefrom to return to their homes without conditions." The entire Resolution will be presented in the final chapter of the book.

I have personally visited several refugee camps and can attest to the abject poverty and denigrative squalor that permeates these camps. I have seen legal land titles to homes and property in the hands of these refugees, but their documents mean nothing to the belligerent, intransigent Zionists who now "own" the land.

It is here, in the midst of these camps that the PLO was born. And it is here that young children squat in the relentless heat and dust of remote camps and dream of a better life and future, if not for themselves, then for their children. It is these children who will become Palestinian Commandoes and Guerillas. Their single goal and objective is to REGAIN THEIR LAND, THEIR HOMES, THEIR COUNTRY.

I now offer a summary of what I consider to be grave injustices to the Palestinian People. Here is an overview of what has taken place thus far in the middle east struggle:

(1) With the exception of 931 miles purchased outright by

the Jews and about 373 miles still in possession of Palestinians, the remaining 11,489 miles of Palestine were acquired by the Jews through the use of physical force and violence.

(2) Approximately 1,500,000 persons now live in forced absence from their homes. They have been replaced by about 2,000,000 Jewish immigrants who have entered the country against the wishes of the original inhabitants.

(3) After the 1967 war all Palestine was conquered and Palestinians who lost lands and properties have lost all their political rights as well.

(4) The "foreign" and sovereign State of Israel was established utilizing Palestinian-owned homes and land.

Regardless of one's personal feelings or philosophy, the facts, numbers, and statistics presented are true. The terrible persecutions carried out against the Jews both prior to World War I and during World War II have in reality little to do with the issue before us. There is no "justification" for any nation or race of people to simply decide they desire or "deserve" another nation's land and property. Never before in the history of civilized man has such an obvious injustice been perpetrated against any nation or people, as the illegal seizure of Palestine by the Zionist leaders of the Jews. There is no historical precedent for any country being "right" or "correct" in taking over another country from its legitimate, original inhabitants. The only comparable act to somewhat parallel this event is the invasion of Afghanistan in 1980 by Russia, and perhaps the previous invasions of Poland, Czechoslovakia and Hungary, also invaded by the "freedom-loving" Marxist regime.

Before any serious dialogue can even begin, this act must be recognized and exposed for what it is, namely, a blatant attack, a military conquest and subsequent occupation of one of the world's nations and people.

Aggression under any pretext is never justifiable, and the great world-conscience must be pricked if and when a measure of redress and acceptable negotiation is to result in bringing about an end to the tragedy of the Middle East Dilemma.

Chapter 3

THE NATURE OF ZIONISM

PERSONS MAKING A serious attempt to grasp the complexities of the mideast Conflict soon realize that Zionism is one of the root causes for the continuing struggle. In Chapters 1 and 2, I made several statements relative to the Zionist Organization and its goal of re-establishing the biblical state of Israel. It would appear impossible to this author for any person, however well-intentioned he may be, to find a solution to the present conflict without some degree of knowledge as to the various aspects of Zionism and its influence on the world as well as Middle Eastern affairs.

I have lectured on Archaeology and the middle east in nearly every major city of America. In all my travels, I have met a mere handful of individuals who were aware of the great importance of Zionism in the ongoing crisis between the Arab People and the Jews. Assuming the reader is among the majority who are in great need of the facts regarding Zionism, I will present an overview of the history, purpose, goals and future of Zionism.

HISTORICAL BACKGROUND OF ZIONISM

Zionism is a product of the Jewish mind, and a full understanding of it requires consideration of the ancient history of the Jews.

In Chapter 1, we learned the Habirus were more likely the

19

ancestors of the Jews. These Habirus came from such divergent places as Ur in Mesopotamia, Mari, Nuzi, Anatolia, Canaan and Egypt. They became the slaves of the Egyptians, but conducted a mass exodus from Egypt between the years 1444 and 1440 B.C. The Biblical record indicates they became a "covenant people" of Yahweh (Hebrew for God, same as Jehovah). Exodus 19:4 tells us they were to be a "kingdom of priests and a holy nation." This covenant society, under the name of Israel, conquered many parts of Palestine, but their conquest was not complete until the reign of King David in 1000 B.C. During the period of the conquest the Israelites were loosely organized as an amphictyony around a religious shrine (the Temple). Under the first King of Israel, King Saul who ruled from 1050 to 1010 B.C., there was no central authority. True central authority began with King David who succeeded Saul in 1000 B.C. This centralized authority continued under David's son, King Solomon, and lasted a total of approximately eighty years.

Various archaeological findings have validated the existence of these three kings. Dr. William F. Albright, world renowned scholar and archaeologist, excavated the fortress/palace of Saul in 1922. The site was known biblically as "Gibeah" (Joshua 15:57) and is today "Tell-El Ful," meaning hill of beans. The remains of one corner of Saul's palace was unearthed by Albright. The palace was not large but well fortified with double defense walls and towers.

Validation of King David as a genuine historical person is unquestioned in light of the numerous archaeological finds such as "David's City" on Mount Ophel near Jerusalem, currently being excavated by the Hebrew University of Jerusalem and the Israel Exploration Society.

As for King Solomon, archaeology has confirmed his chariot city at Gezer, including an underground spring beneath the city. Excavations from 1960-1978 exposed the outer walls and gates of Gezer, as well as horse stalls, feeding troughs and grain bins. (See I Kings 9:16-17.) The remains of Solomon's copper mines and smelter works have been found near the Jordan River (I Kings 7:38-45). Other stables belonging to Solomon have been found at Megiddo, and Gath (I Kings 10:26).

Once again I encourage the reader to note the archaeological references listed in the back of this book, and to make oneself aware of this important material which substantiates the historical narratives of the Bible.

After Solomon, the Kingdom was divided into two minor kingdoms, Judah in the south, and Israel in the north. The total life of the United Monarchy was some ninety years, including the reign of Saul. This represents the total time during which the process of creating a distinct nationality could have been in progress. We have already noted the historical background of the fall of the two states and the dispersion of their inhabitants. After the fall of the two states, and an attempt to mount a return to Israel had failed, the Jews eventually scattered all over the world. Those who did remain in the mideast were easily absorbed into the Semitic communities, although some did retain their own Jewish faith.

Those Jews who continued to live in the European countries were often, after the rise of Christianity, subjected to persecution and discrimination as presented in Chapter I. During their early days of captivity in both Assyria and Babylonia, the Jews cherished their memories of the former theocratic state and longed to re-establish that state. The continued persecution created the first Zionist Congress in 1897 at Basil, Switzerland. The immediate causes which led Theodore Herzle to convene this Congress are well known, and we have already touched upon that background in the first portion of the book. It was at this Congress that the Zionist Organization was formed and charged with the task of working towards the realization of the Zionist programme.

THE NAME OF ZION OR ZIONIST

The word Zion, pronounced "tsiyon," means the top of a ridge, and was used to mean a citadel. The Arabic root is used in the same sense, but in addition it denotes the saddle place on the back of a horse. The Arab word is "saza." As a proper name, the word was used as the name of the Jebusite stronghold on the southern part of the eastern hill of Jerusalem.

David captured this stronghold some 3000 years ago. The story is found in II Samuel 5:7. After the capture, David transferred his capital from Hebron to Jerusalem and brought the Ark of the Covenant to the city. Later, the Temple, which housed the Ark, was built on the same site. Eventually, the name Zion was used for the whole of the eastern hill, and figuratively for the whole of Jerusalem, even for the whole people of Israel. (See Isaiah 1:8 and Isaiah 1:27.)

Zion came to represent not only the theocratic state, but also the spiritual ideals of the invisible God of Israel, who dwelt in the Temple, within the Holy of Holies.

ZIONISM IN THE 19TH CENTURY

The word "Zionism" was coined in the 19th century as a result of persecution, and was intended to convey the desire of many Jews to re-establish Palestine as the old state of Israel. This is known as *POLITICAL ZIONISM.* This desire for the old state of Israel was purely political and, from the beginning, no desire to return to the ethical and moral teachings practiced by the Jews under the Mosaic Law was expressed. There were some Jews who envisioned a restoration of the old ethical life as recorded in Psalm 15, but they were a definite minority. Their philosophy or teaching was known as spiritual or cultural Zionism. The return to Palestine conveyed both the political and religious desires to a third group of Jews. The late Martin Buber, Professor at the Hebrew University, was probably one of the better known spokesmen for this third group. In an attempt to justify Zionism on ethical grounds, and to support the demand for the creation of a "second Israel," he said on March 14, 1946, given in evidence before the Anglo-American Committee:

"This explains why Judaism did not simply create another national movement of the European type, but a unique one, a "Zionism."

THE NATURE OF ZIONISM

Professor Buber seemed to be an honest thinker and a genuine seeker of peace. He described Zionism in 1946 as a "unique" national movement. Obviously, he must have thought of it in ideal terms. For he stated in another part of his evidence that the Jewish community was confronted with the task of establishing in Canaan a model and just society which was later on interpreted by the prophets as "obliging the community to send streams of social and political justice throughout the world." But these early Zionist "prophets" had not experienced the functioning of Zionism in a sovereign Zionist state. This experience is now open and revealed for the entire world to see, examine, and to judge. It would be of interest to examine the question whether political Zionism, in its present form, can be justified on any grounds whatsoever! We might also question whether it is good for Israel, its neighbors the Palestinians and the Arabs, and for the whole world. It is time for us to see what Zionism, by its very nature, implies in real practice.

In the fall of 1980, my wife and I were returning to Cairo, Egypt, on an Egyptian airline from a visit to Abu Simbel. We were seated next to a Jewish man from Miami, Florida. The discussion soon centered on Palestine, Zionism and situation ethics. After openly claiming to be a modern-day Zionist, he quickly became defensive, curt, belligerent and out of control. I then suggested it was the Palestinians who were currently being persecuted and not the Jews. The immediate response was as if to ignite a skyrocket within the cabin of a commercial airliner, an Egyptian airline at that! This U.S. citizen stated he believed in and was fully supportive of the occupation of Palestine and condoned *THE KILLING OF ARAB WOMEN AND CHILDREN* in order for the Jews to retain their Jewish state! Is this not the theme of constant propaganda promoted around the world by Zionists through any and all means of media and communication? Was not the killing of innocent women and children, old men and women, the heart and soul of the so-called "Holocaust" carried out against these self-same Jews? Yet hear their words, their oaths and dedication to perpetuate their stolen nation even at the expense of the innocent! I recognize that not all Jews are as abrasive or in support of such injustice and travesty, but likewise the greater proportion of the Arab People are not the bloodthirsty murderers so often portrayed to the world by this present-day Zionist government now ruling Palestine. But I can truthfully state that of the many Zionists I have talked with over the past fifteen years, nearly all have echoed those sentiments of the American Zionist.

But perhaps even more alarming was this man's statement he would support the Zionist occupation, "even if it means opposing the laws and political policies of my own country." Herein lies the most dangerous concept of the Zionist philosophy, the fact that a Zionist Jew living outside Israel as a citizen of another state is bound to have his political loyalties divided between Israel and the state or country of which he is a citizen. All citizens of all countries bear political rights and responsibilities. Their first and primary responsibilities are for and to their own parent country. Yet the Zionist Jew has a dual loyalty, first to the state of Israel, and secondly his native country. Dual loyalty is inherent in Zionism. And when this "allegiance" is organized into pressure groups, it can be most serious and embarrassing both for the individual and his country. This is especially true when one considers the extremely non-ethical conditions prevailing in our world. Since Zionist Jews live in various countries, they can easily become agents for specific world powers in order to create in their home countries, the unrest and disharmony desired by those world powers. It takes little or no imagination to recognize the turmoil and destruction which can occur if Zionist leaders desire such unrest to occur for any political reasons whatsoever.

Zionism can potentially create the opportunities for provoking trouble in any part of our world. A Zionist state has loyal adherents all over the world who are always able to take shelter behind their "second" citizenship, and such adherents might be easily tempted in our unethical world to act as agents for any superior power. How could any Zionist be trusted with any position of security or national defense, if indeed his first loyalty is not to his own country? How can anyone swear allegiance to two countries simultaneously? I can think of nothing more destructive for world peace than to permit just such a "dual-citizen" structure to exist in the world community. Yet the largest concentrations of Zionist Jews outside Israel live within the territories under the sovereignty or under the sphere of influence of one of the two major world powers. I suggest this fact increases dramatically the dangers we have discussed regarding a major conflict between these super-powers.

Recognizing that many Zionists reside in the United States, we can perhaps understand why America's political leaders have made questionable, if not reckless decisions regarding U.S. foreign policy due to the influence of Zionist political leaders and lobbying. A cursory examination of Middle East decisions and policy from the mid-1950's including the last two decades reveals a host of "trade-off" deals initiated by the last four Presidents, their cabinets and Congress. The majority of these were to the detriment of the United States and precip-itated the present alienation of the United States from the Arab world and the OPEC leaders who are now using their control of oil as a bargaining chip to attempt to induce American policy to demonstrate a more even-handed attitude towards the Palestinian People. Our politicians have contin-ually voted and advanced pro-Israeli policy to avoid the wrath of the "Jewish Vote." One can only wonder what policies would be forthcoming if there were such a group known as the "Russian Vote" or lobby. Would we then hear these same politicians espousing the Marxist philosophy and rhetoric?

The fact that dual citizen Zionists do indeed reside in America can account for the U.S. policy of the past 32 years amounting to total support and endorsement of Israel despite the obvious injustices and inequities perpetrated against the Palestinian Arabs. I believe this is the explanation for the purposeful animosity now existing between the United States and powerful Arab Nations whose history has been support-ive of American goals and foreign policy except our "blank check" policy with Israel.

The important question as to the citizenship of any individ-ual must be considered in light of this "dual citizenship" issue. Is it "Un-American" to ask a citizen to swear his first and only allegiance to his native land rather than a second country which might represent his personal religious, cultural, or political persuasion? As an American citizen and former Marine, I have no difficulty pledging my first allegiance and concern for my own native country. It is America and its citizens of all the ages past who have fought and sustained the many rights, pleasures, and opportunities its citizens can enjoy. It is to this same great country that every citizen, Jew or Gentile, native or immigrant, must be dedicated and devoted. NO SECOND OR THIRD COUNTRY MUST TAKE PRECEDENCE ABOVE HER!

A Zionist state of Israel, however small in area, is bound to think of itself as an empire with a substantial number of its citizenship living outside its borders and within "other countries." The assumption which naturally follows is that the Zionist leaders can exert considerable influence upon the internal policies of those "other" countries. Indeed, they have demonstrated the ability to exploit the wealth and power of those countries by means of control of mass media and communication within those countries (the U.S. included). With the ability to exert pressure and influence upon the policies of other countries, the present Israeli government continues its policy of expansionism and new settlements upon Arab lands.

The unpleasant characteristics we have just related need not all operate in one direction, that is, the state of Israel penetrating other countries. There may well exist wealthy Zionists living outside Israel who are anxious to exploit Israel's sovereignty to their own personal advantage. In either case, this unique "nationalism" can be harmless only in a very ethical world, or if Zionism confines itself to spiritual activities and cultural concerns and abandons completely all political objectives. Realistically speaking, the world society is null and void of ethical considerations or moral responsibility in its political proposals, national goals and endeavors. Ours is a world of political expediency, a world whose political leaders espouse Dialectical Materialism and Totalitarianism. Freedom and Democracy are threatened from all sides; Marx and Lenin have replaced Washington and Lincoln as the founders of liberty and justice. The need of the hour for the great Republic of America is for every citizen of varying ethnic origin and background to pledge anew his allegiance to the goals and history of America, that this nation might withstand the onslaught of vain philosophies which promise prosperity to all, but in reality bring turmoil, bloodshed, and national destruction. Thus, there can be no valid justification nor acceptance of "dual citizenship" among concerned citizens.

It is probable the early founders of the Zionist Organization never envisioned that Zionism would acquire the evil characteristics presented thus far in our discussion. But human nature, being a very real part of every human organization, renders that organization unpredictable and at best, unaffected by past history or human experience. Do we suppose the founders of the American nation would have ever envisioned us willingly supportive of the 'Theft of a Nation'? Would they be supportive of a faltering foreign policy of the President and the Congress of the United States which proclaim "human rights" the ultimate issue, yet deny those same human rights to entire nations by supporting the violent overthrow of those nations by Socio-Communistic Humanists who, once in power, foment hate and revolution against that self-same President and his Congress? Is this not precisely what has happened in our support of the occupation of Palestine?

The United States will face a long and difficult road to overcome a worldwide image of indecisiveness and weakness as a direct result of the compromise and naivete of our Presidents and their Congress.

ANTI-SEMITISM INCLUDES ARABS

Chapter 1 dealt with the origin of the Arab and the Jew. Both were Semites, therefore, if one is "anti-semitic" today, he is then, against five ancient peoples including the Arabs! This phrase has been loosely used to incriminate and indict those who oppose the Zionist dream, or speak of the injustices being perpetrated against the Palestinian People. We have already discussed the cruel and criminal attitudes and actions against the European Jews of the past. It is at this point in history when the first misapplication of the term "semitic" and "anti-semitic" was used. Remember, more than one million Palestinian Arabs still living in Palestine are Semites! They remain today, as they have remained from the beginning, vehemently opposed to the Jewish occupation of their country. This opposition cannot be termed anti-semitism. Semites are not against Semites. Rather, the Semitical Arabs are at odds with the Zionist Jews who continue to espouse their "right to conquest" and a "national homeland" as embodied in the Zionist Manifesto of 1897. If the Arab people are anti-semitic, then native American Indians were and are "anti-American" for resisting the occupation and settlement of their land by the immigrating European pilgrims and subsequent pioneer settlers.

IMMIGRATION VS EMIGRATION

More and more Jews are realizing that Zionism, as practiced at present, is not only detrimental to their own interests, but it also completely contradicts the best in true Jewish faith and tradition. Thousands of Jews are leaving Israel at an unprecedented rate, disillusioned with the Zionist dream of a peaceful homeland. The promised utopia simply has not materialized. Although the number emigrating (leaving Israel) appears to be a small fraction of the total population of Israel's 3.2 million Jews, the exodus is increasing at an alarming rate of 2,000 a month according to a recent estimate by a special Knesset (parliament) committee. The term or Hebrew word for emigration is 'yerida' and implies desertion and a lowering of standards.

An Israeli psychologist offered the following reason for the exodus: "It is the death of idealism. Nothing works anymore. There is a feeling of helplessness, that you can't influence any decisions." The Jerusalem Post: "People are leaving who are sick and tired of high taxes, rudeness, over 130 percent inflation, alarming headlines, clowning politicians and reserve duty."

Nearly half who leave settle in the United States. The American Embassy in Israel has been issuing immigrant visas to Israelis at a rate of 2,000 per year since 1975. But nonimmigrant visa applications for visiting the U.S. have doubled in five years, to more than 80,000 in 1979 alone. No one knows how many Israelis traveling with such visas, stay on in the U.S. illegally. An estimated 400,000 Israeli citizens live in America, and 250,000 to 300,000 of this number reside in New York City. America has a Jewish community of approximately 5.4 million. Many feel the current Israeli government and politicians have lost their true Jewish identity. Basic humane tenets no longer apply to what the government is doing, including blowing up homes of West Bank Arabs for stoning Israeli cars.

Compounding the situation is the startling fact that immigration (those arriving from other countries to live in Israel), the lifeblood of the Jewish state, is ebbing. Since 1948 1.7 million immigrants have been absorbed from the Diaspora of Jews scattered around the world. Immigration was down 31 percent for the first five months of the year 1980 when compared with the same months of the year 1979.

Of those who do immigrate to Israel, the larger number are young Zionists not informed of the failure of the past and present governments to establish the homeland. The Central Bureau of Statistics estimates that 40 perent of these leave after a few years. (An excellent article on Emigration from Israel can be found in U.S. News and World Report, June, 1980, from which I have researched the preceding statistics and information.)

Religious Jews have often shared with me their own persecution and injustices carried out against them by the Political Zionists. Few religious Jews, if any, would have envisioned the State of Israel recognizing the Communist Party as an official and legal "party" of the people in Israel, but nonetheless, it is so. Many Jewish leaders blame the orthodox and religious Jews of the past for their persecution and disfavor. Many have been imprisoned and harassed, especially those concerned with the unethical treatment of the Arab People.

It is unbelievable that the people who have contributed so much to the spiritual thinking of the world should be hypnotized by the glare of temporary political and military power, thus turning away from the eternal power of Justice and Righteousness. Worldly empires have come and gone, but the invisible empire of Truth and Justice is eternal. It is time that all Jews throughout the world realize they have not survived because of the military feats of their ancient judges or kings, but because of the moral and ethical teachings of their humble prophets. Aggression, belligerency, and injustice as embodied by the current Zionist Israeli government, can only hinder the search for a lasting peace in the Middle East.

Chapter 4

POLITICAL REALITIES AND RAMIFICATIONS

DURING THE LONG sixty year period of conflict and struggle in pursuit of control of Palestine, a great number of political, social, economical and historical occurrences have emerged. The important effects and ramifications of the mideast drama need to be stated and considered if we are to arrive at an honest, impartial conclusion.

The various political realities discussed in this chapter represent only those realities I selected as the more obvious and weighty, and in no way do I infer they are the only results or realities. The following effects are without boundary restriction and affect all the nations of the world in one way or another.

(1) The occupation of Palestine by political Zionists has artificially created a new political boundary by planting a totally foreign element within a territory which was, more or less, homogeneously populated. The new Zionist element is foreign in culture, language, religious persuasion, and group objectives.

The reaction to this foreign body has been total rejection by Palestinian natives. The by-product of their rejection has been the continuation of mutually bitter hatred and enmity on the part of Arab and Jew. It is ironic and sad that this hatred emanates in the land from which the first message of universal peace and love was first announced to the world some two thousand years ago. The quantity of hatred engendered has been so vast that it has spilled over, covering the surface of the earth.

Nations of the world look daily to the mideast to note the current status which will in some manner affect their own government whether by direct confrontation due to political treaties, or indirect involvement such as the purchase of oil and fuel supplies from a dwindling market which lies situated in the dead center of the conflict between Arab and Jew.

(2) The continued occupation of Palestine has served to resurrect the old and unused Hebrew language at a time when world progress demands a decrease in language differences. The purpose of establishing this language was in the hope that it would act as an adhesive plaster to bind artificially, into one nationality based on religion, all the Jews of the world who belong to diverse nationalities. This hope has not been realized except for the relatively small number of Jews who imigrated to Israel. The attempt has resulted in the appearance of the phenomenon of "dual loyalty" and in the creation of a small state based on "religion." Both results have contributed to the lack of progress to world peace and feed the flames of prejudice and intolerance between Arabs and Jews, Presidents, Kings, and Nations.

(3) The Occupation has divided the nations of the earth into two distinct camps: one supporting Israel and the other, in support of the Palestinians. It is notable that those who support Israel are primarily considered to be "Christian" nations who, in their own immediate past, persecuted the Jews. Germany seems obsessed with attempting to "rectify" the hatred and full scale rage exacted against the European Jews during World War II by pledging their support of the political state of Israel. Great Britain and France now posture as steadfast allies to the Israeli state as if their open hostility and disdain for the Jews of their own countries had never been discovered. This hostility was easily recognizable during the war, and continues in our present day. Admittedly, the world community has chosen sides not on the basis of moral right and the pursuit of justice, but rather the same mercenary spirit of political expediency. But nevertheless, the world camp is divided by the Palestinian issue.

(4) The occupation threatens to precipitate a third world war which may involve the use of nuclear weapons. The harm posed to the entire world population is obvious and needs no deliberation. Yet one good thing may result from such an eventuality if indeed humanity were to survive, and that is the world will have learned an unforgettable lesson at great cost, the lesson being that "injustice is the reason for conflict." This lesson can still be learned at little cost to the world if they will but heed the teaching of Jesus Christ and His great guidelines for true and lasting peace through application of the "Golden Rule."

(5) The conflict is causing many honest persons to reflect seriously as to what is truly the best economic system for the world. We must decide and determine if it is a good thing for the human race that the power of "money" with all of its potential visible and invisible pressures and abuses, should be allowed to dominate world events, with the object of supporting vested interests or injustice in places around the world. Once again every world citizen must determine the answer to this question: Is justice, right and truth simply a matter of material and military success resultant of monetary underwriting, or popular acceptance of a common teaching?

The occupation of Palestine by the political Zionists teeters on the brink of the sponsorship of a religious war. The Palestinians have thus far maintained their conflict and dispute is not with Judaism, but the Zionist philosophy and its ramifications. But as more and more land is expropriated, and new settlements continue to sprout in the cities, towns and villages where there has been only Palestine Arabs for thousands of years, the entire world of Islam is beginning to speak of the conflict in terms of a "Jihaad" or holy war. Even the Zionist leaders of the current Israeli government "quote" various scriptural passages from the Bible as evidence and justification for their "right" to possess the land, and to dispossess the Palestinian Arabs.

(6) The fact that Western Christians are supporting an obvious injustice makes Christianity, with all the idealism it claims for itself, suspect in the eyes of millions of non-Christians. Already, mission work and evangelistic efforts of Christian Churches have been and are being, greatly diminished.

Some of the major evangelical denominations who have established long and effective ministries among the Arab people, are now finding it near impossible to continue their efforts due to the distrust and dislike generated by this well advertised support of Israel by many fundamental denominations. I know of four schools no longer operative within Palestine because of this very same attitude. Yet the fundamental ethical principle in Christianity is "love". But love can have no meaning unless it begins with justice. While studying the tenets of Islam, I found it more than interesting to learn that Islam speaks little of love, but rather concentrates on justice under all conditions. Yet true Christianity in its purest form was originated as a way of life, an attitude and philosophy of life which causes every man to consider right and wrong, truth and non-truth, before commencing any action towards another human being. I will have a great deal more to say on this important reality in the chapter dealing with Christianity and Biblical Prophecy.

(7) The Mid-East crisis is causing some major world powers to recognize the "right of conquest" and threatens to take our world back to the disastrous military and political instability which existed before World War I. This retrogression should cause each of us to be greatly alarmed, for it could well lead us backwards to conditions which produced the "might makes right" slogan and the associate attitude that force should decide the right for existence. Under present world conditions and with our modern technology, the world's citizenry will not continue to accept two standards of justice; one governing international relations and the other regulating individual behavior. It is because of the conflict between these standards that we see individuals around the world taking the law and a desire for justice into their own hands. They are attempting to impose their own ideas of justice and as a result, are called criminals or terrorists by some segments of society. But I must ask, are they indeed any more criminal in their methods than those governments who use force to support prevailing injustice in any of its many forms? Injustice and deceit are no less an evil simply because it is carried out collectively or by elected politicians rather than the world citizenry.

THE CURRENT POLITICAL STATUS

The United States has historically supported the right of a Jewish state and homeland, but not at the expense and injustice to the Palestinian People. Despite disagreement with Israel over settlements and land grabbing, the official commitment of the U.S. government to the Jewish nation remains unchanged. America has maintained special ties with Israel from its beginning and as of September 1982, will have provided the tiny state with over 4.3 billion dollars in economic aid and nearly 12.9 billion in military assistance. Military aid consists of about 7.7 billion in loans and the remainder in grants.

Every U.S. President since 1948 has voiced support for Israel. Key statements over the past 30 years include:

PRESIDENT TRUMAN, October 28, 1948, five months after the Jewish state was born: "It is my desire to help build in Palestine a strong, prosperous, free and democratic state. It must be large enough, free enough, and strong enough to make its people self-supporting and secure."

PRESIDENT EISENHOWER, January 5, 1957: "We have shown our dedication to the principle that force shall not be used internationally for any aggressive purpose and that the integrity and independence of the Middle East shall remain inviolate."

PRESIDENT KENNEDY, May 8, 1963: "We support the security of both Israel and her neighbors."

PRESIDENT JOHNSON, May 23, 1967: "I wish to say what three presidents have said before...the U.S. is firmly committed to the support of the political independence and territorial integrity of all the nations of the Mideast."

PRESIDENT NIXON, June 1, 1972: "I reiterate the American people's commitment to the survival of the Israeli state."

PRESIDENT FORD, September 10, 1974: "We are committed to Israel's survival and security."

PRESIDENT CARTER, January 23, 1979: "Our firm commitment to Israel's survival and security is rooted in our deepest convictions and in our knowledge of the strategic importance to our own nation of a stable Middle East."

PRESIDENT REAGAN: Has thus far repeated a similar view.

President Jimmy Carter was the first President to make the verbal pledge into a diplomatic document. In a "memorandum of agreement" signed March 26, 1979, between the United States and Israel as part of the Camp David package, Washington (that's you and me) formally promised to endeavor to come to Israel's aid with military and economic assistance if the peace treaty with Egypt is violated. A second memorandum commits the U.S. for 15 years to supply Israel with oil at world prices if Israel is cut off from its normal sources.

This accord was designed to persuade Israel to return captured oil wells in the Sinai Desert to Egypt, the original and rightful owners of the wells. The Carter administration also provided Israel with THREE BILLION DOLLARS to finance its withdrawal from the Sinai, and 800 million in grants to relocate airfields and the rest will be a ten year loan. Israel already owes the United States over SIXTEEN BILLION DOLLARS!

Since the 1967 war, political leaders of the U.S. have altered perceptably their views of total unconditional support for the state of Israel. There are numerous reasons for these alterations, but we will limit our discussion to the more current and familiar reasons.

FAILURE OF THE CAMP DAVID PEACE PLAN

Though there appears to be an acceptable peace between Egypt and Israel, the agreement stands in constant danger of unravelling due to the fact that all three major parties, Egypt,

Israel and the United States, negotiated plans and proposals, withdrawals and boundary lines without even the slighest consideration, consultation, or communication with the Palestinian People!

It is true that former President Anwar Sadat, for whom I had the utmost respect and admiration, insisted throughout deliberations that a pivotal point for the success of their "treaty" would be a just and equitable solution to the Palestinian issue. It is here that Menachen Begin and his cabinet have vowed absolute resistance.

To the Egyptians, their suggestion that the 1.3 million Palestinians of the West Bank and the Gaza Strip be enabled to return to their former homes, land and country, and assume their own "home rule" means the Palestinians should be given a full range of powers...the same powers that Israel's military government now exercises over the occupied lands. Israeli spokesmen express fear that such a formula *MIGHT* lead to a Palestinian state, which they reject as a threat to their own future and security. Mr. Begin has offered only severely restricted local rule over such things as education, health, and ordinary municipal affairs. Remember, if you will, we are talking about the right of self-determination supposedly granted every nation of people whether in the United States, Africa, or Palestine.

Palestinian Arabs living within the state of Israel and those scattered throughout the Mideast countries have waited over thirty years for a just settlement of the issue by the major nations of the world. As Mayor Mohammed Milhem of the town of Halhoul said,

> *"We saw what happened for thirty years by relying on the sympathy of the world...nothing."*

The Camp David accords concluded and signed by Sadat, Begin and Carter, CALL FOR HOME RULE FOR ARABS LIVING IN THEIR OWN OCCUPIED LANDS! That is over one million people! But instead of meaning self-rule and independence, Israel interprets this to mean watered-down continued control of territory it seized by force during the 1967 Arab-Israeli War. The Israeli government not only refuses to initiate action agreed to in "good faith" as regards the Palestinians, but insist on calling the West Bank by its Biblical names, Judea and Samaria. Again, if you will recall our first two chapters, you will note these two names were nonexistent until 1000 B.C. It is especially distressing to note the use of Biblical texts and titles as some kind of "proof" of ownership, when in many cases those using the Biblical claims do so from a purely political and expedient attitude rather than a true belief, practice or adherence to the Biblical teachings.

New American policy was reflected when President Carter made clear our goals included the insurance of Israel's security, and for the first time, to help West Bank and Gaza Arabs obtain legitimate rights in a homeland of their own. Thus, the Camp David accord now totters on the brink of disaster due to lack of instigation and the failure to consider the needs and desires of the Palestinians.

Virtually all Arab leaders of the West Bank and Gaza reject the self-rule plan laid out at Camp David. They ask for and demand self-determination which will result in independence. From my personal travels and excavations in Palestine, I have found an absolute unanimity among professional and nonprofessional Palestinians, rich and poor, and that unanimity is centered in their determination to cast off what they perceive as a yoke, the Israeli military and civilian control and occupation of their land and their homes.

Because of past deception and deceit, most Palestinians have no trust whatsoever of any agreement whether made by Egyptians, Jews, or Americans. They are convinced the present Jewish state wishes only to force the remaining Palestinians within Israel to leave. Karim Khalaf, Mayor of Ramallah, speaks for many Palestinians when he says:

"The Israelis don't want peace. They want a piece of land."

AMERICAN DISENCHANTMENT CONTINUES

Because of our blind and ill-considered support of Israel, anti-American hostility is growing rapidly throughout the Mideast. On numerous occasions I have been questioned by Arabs seeking to determine why it is we hate and dislike them. An Arab doctor in Nablus said,

"People on the West Bank believe everything is in the hands of America. If America withdraws support of Israel, it will only then begin to consider us."

The Saudis, the Syrians, Lebanese, Iraquis and Libyans are turning to the world's "pariah" for power, the Soviet Union, for both political and military aid. They feel America has "written them off" as evidenced by the U.S. stance in support of the continued occupation of Palestine. Indeed, if one is to judge by past and present attitudes and actions of the United States, the Palestinians have been adjudged "guilty" of being the agressor in the Mideast conflict. Yet I must remind the reader once again of the *FACTS*; it is the Arab who has been driven from his home, his land and native country; it is the Arab who has suffered the humiliation of being an outcast, a refugee, literally a nation without a country. I find it difficult to accept the illogical deduction that the Palestinian Arabs who are the true victims of the dillemma, are somehow reckoned to be the perepetrators of their own persecution. Those Palestinians who still live within the state of Israel have no weapons, no arms with which to "wage war" against the Israeli military which governs their cities and villages, especially against an Israeli army that likes to proclaim its super power status in terms of armament and advanced weapons capabilities.

Despite the constant propaganda maintained by the Israeli press which portrays the "local" Arabs living within Israel as happy and quite satisfied with their current status, such is not the case. One must be cautious in assuming the vehement resistance to the occupation is primarily limited to those Palestinians residing outside of Israel, for the will to resist and to fight the occupation with whatever means available is persistent among all Palestinians. In the pessimistic words of one Arab journalist as to any chance of a peaceful settlement:

*"Every individual, every mother, all are ready to sacrifice
to gain our freedom."*

One significant event which served as the catalyst for the
growing hostility towards America was President Carter's
"reversal" in a crucial United Nations resolution passed in
1979. A statement condemning the Israeli-settlement policy
on the West Bank was at first voted for and supported by our
Amassador to the U.N., McDonald Henry. When news of the
vote reached Israel, the Israeli government bristled and spoke
of a "betrayal" of the U.S. pledge of support, while the
Palestinians thought at long last someone had finally recognized their plight. Quickly, the oft-denied Jewish political
influence or backlash made its way to our nation's capital and
the oval office. Carter quickly issued a statement disavowing
our previous vote and implying our Ambassador and his aides
had "made a mistake" and were not apprised of all the facts
before casting their vote. This naked capitulation to the
Jewish power brokers in Israel and the United States during a
Presidential election year was the final straw which vaporized
any remaining possibility of American impartiality and
credibility.

THE RUSSIAN CONNECTION

The Soviet Union stands to profit more than any other country as a direct result of the continuing conflict. Presently,
Russia is playing the role of Arab benefactor and guardian,
the only true friend who "understands" the grievous wrongs
perpetrated against the Palestinian People. The Russians have
gained appreciably in status and credibility, for they have
from the beginning and are at present continuing to supply
arms and training of volunteers in military tactics. They miss
no opportunity to appear openly supportive of the Palestinian
Cause. Of course, it should be obvious even to the more
casual student of world history that the Russian motives have
little to do with a real desire for "justice," or a driving passion
for the abolishment of the many inequities and injustices

exacted against the Palestinian Arabs. It is important to look for a more self-serving reason behind the support and rhetoric of a nation now itself guilty of occupying another nation and people, as communist Russia now seeks to exterminate the Afghani people who resist their "occupation" of Afghanistan. One need only look closely at a map of the Middle East showing the locations of Russian troops or military "advisers" to know what Russia's true motives are, and how their gamble has paid off for the advancement of Marxism and the Communist philosophy.

THE PALESTINIANS ARE NOT COMMUNISTS

I think it is important to dispel the current popular propaganda that the Arabs are either communists or ignorant "dupes" and mere puppets who do the bidding for the Kremlin. First of all, the religious teaching of the Arab people absolutely precludes the Marxist philosophy from ever becoming a credible or viable part of the Arab culture. By far the majority of Arabs are Moslems or Mohammedans who practice the ancient tenets of Islam. The term Islam means "submission to God." The very heart of the Islamic religion is the submission of followers to the will of God. Founded in the seventh century after Christ in Arabia, Islam had converts from Spain to India within the middle of the eighth century. No other faith has been so successful in Africa or in Arabic speaking lands.

Islam's sacred book is the Koran; its temples, mosques; its requirements include: faith in Allah (God) and in Mohammed as his prophet; prayer five times daily; adherence to the requirements of Islam, and good works. Moslems must practice prayer and fasting, give alms, and make a pilgrimage to Mecca at least once in a lifetime.

With this understanding of Islam, the charge that "the Arabs are really communists in disguise" is exposed in all its absurdity. THERE IS NO WAY the many Moslem countries of the world will ever embrace communism as a philosophy or way of life. The Moslem's very life is inextricably entwined with his religion. His religion is not something "he does" but rather, something *he is.*

We need reminding that Russia is the world capital for the propagation of the communist philosophy. Whether one considers the original composition of Frederick Engels and Karl Marx, co-founders of communism, or the refined and expanded ideology of Lenin and Stalin, communism is based upon Dialectical Materialism, and is absolutely GODLESS! Therefore, there is no compatibility between true Islam and communism, between Russian and Arab in religion or convictions, values or philosopohy.

President Anwar Sadat of Egypt effectively throttled the old propaganda slogan rather well when he unceremoniously ejected all Russians from Egyptian soil immediately after the Egyptians crossed the Suez Canal and regained the Negev in the Yom Kippur War of 1973. Men who worship the one true God, men who pray to Him five times per day, and men who truly care for others can never qualify as "comrades" of communism.

The second charge frequently expressed is that the Palestinian Arabs are being used by Russia for its own goals and objectives. Again, this is a total untruth. The Palestinians and the other Arab countries have accepted Russian aid and arms for one simple reason: THERE WAS NO OTHER SOURCE OF HELP FORTHCOMING! The United States has repeatedly declined requests for aid from the principle Mideast Arab countries due to our "binding relationship" to the state of Israel and Zionism. Even as this book is written tremendous pressure is being brought to bear on the administration of President Reagan and the Congress for proprosing to sell military weapons and aircraft to Saudi, Arabia. It would seem that the U.S. government has accepted the ridiculous idea that Israel only has a right to be armed and supplied to defend their sovereignty against all aggression. It is this same irrational attitude and policy which has forced many of our pro-American Arab nations into the Russian camp. They have and will continue to accept the Russian aid, but not their philosophy.

In my opinion, it is the Arabs who have "used" the Russians to accomplish their goals of economic and military parody with the Israeli state, rather than the aforementioned scenario. To believe otherwise is to be deceived by current propaganda or demonstrates a severe lack of knowledge and comprehension of the Arab mind and religion.

THE U.S.A. VS. THE U.S.S.R.

In discussing the impact of the instability of the Middle East upon these two countries, it is necessary to begin by recalling the various attitudes and actions of both countries in the immediate past.

(a) The first time the U.S.A. became involved in the Palestinian problem was during the first World War in 1917 when then-President Woodrow Wilson gave his consent to the issue of the Balfour Declaration. American history reveals the reasoning behind his decision of support was political expediency tempered with sincere sympathy for the Jews.

(b) Regardless of Russian policies under the Czars, Russia became openly involved in the Palestine problem only when the scheme for partition was being discussed at the 1947 meeting of the United Nations. The U.S.S.R. then shocked the Arab world by voting for the first time with the Americans in supporting the partition. Indeed, it is a little known fact that, according to Ezer Weizman, former Minister of Defense in his book "The Battle for Peace," without the support of Communist Czechoslovakia and their "gift" of four Messerschmitt 109 fighter planes, the new "state of Israel" would have collapsed from the attacking Egyptian army. The communists were the very first to "recognize" Israel as a state. Why? Why would the communists suddenly decide to support a nation of European immigrants in an already occupied country? The answer to this question becomes obvious upon close examination of the current crisis. The partition decision and the chaos and terror, plus the local wars it precipitated made it possible for the Russians to inject themselves into the affairs of the Middle East. This welcomed opportunity of adventurism would never have occurred so easily if the area had remained stable and peaceful. The process is in a state of continuation, and it is for each individual to ascertain the extent of the Russian influence and power gained by the setting up of the Jewish state of Israel.

(c) None should be blind to the fact that both super powers have vested interests in the developments of the Mideast Conflict. In the eyes of the world, the only difference between the two powers at present is that the United States, shamefully, is seen as supporting an injustice while the Russians seem to be aligned on the side of true justice, irregardless of their real motives or political strategy. It is the same strategy used by the communists in the various trouble spots around the world. Although most thinking Americans recognize the veiled hyprocisy of Russian concern for the down-trodden and dispossessed as cosmetic covering to accompany total infiltration, these same American citizens must face up to the realization that the U.S. position of supporting the Theft of A Nation is absolutely wrong and morally hypocritical. But why does the United States continue to remain involved in such an apparent injustice? In seeking to find the answer to this question I have personally interviewed more than 500 Americans over the past eight years. I asked them why they thought our government should support Israel against the Palestinians. The answers are revealing for some are of a religious or humane nature, while still others are purely political and mercenary, a seeming contradiction of motives.

One of the most frequent responses I received was the thought that the Jews would be a better hedge against communist influence of the Mideast. A typical presentation of this motive was given by a Mr. Hunter, an American clergyman. He gave the following speech to a group of Arab intellectuals on July 15, 1947, in Jerusalem. This was prior to the partition and the establishment of the Israeli state in 1948.

Mr. Hunter represented a group of American clergy who were quite vocal in their strong support for Zionism and had signed a petition to the White House asking the President to support Zionism. They each had circulated numerous pamphlets as well as radio tapes in support of their "position." A resume of the views expressed by Mr. Hunter to the Arab group was published at the time in Arabic in a school magazine, "Sawt-el-Kulliyeh." The following is a translation without comment of that resume as published:

> *"As a group we are greatly interested in world peace;*
> *at the same time we recognize that the Middle East is a*

very important and sensitive center which can have paramount influence on the peace we seek to establish. For this reason we are anxious that communism should not be permitted to operate in the Middle East. From our investigation and research we have come to the conclusion that the social and political systems in the Arab world, which are not much different from the feudalism of the Middle Ages, are not able to prevent communism from overrunning the area if it so decides to do so one day.

"On the other hand, Zionism is a socialist movement. It differs from communism in that it is democratic, while communism is a dictatorship. We therefore see in Zionism and in its methods the only hope for shielding the Middle East against communism because it offers the people of this part of the world a social system which they can accept, and which will protect them from the dangers of communism. This is the main reason why we support Zionism. The second reason is of a humane character. We sympathize with the Jews because of the suffering to which they have been subjected as a result of persecution."

At this point, Mr. Hunter's attention was called to a speech made by the former Russian Ambassador to the U.N., in which he freely and openly supported Zionism as did this group of clergy. Mr. Hunter replied that if the Russian Ambassador really meant what he said, then this would be the only weak point in his (Mr. Hunter's) argument. It was then that those in attendance responded that nothing would make the Middle East a center for communism except the success of Zionism in attaining their goals and objectives. This same message has been expressed to the United States Secretary of State during the past five Presidencies. Few seem to be aware of the true tenets of Zionism, and still fewer astute politicians seem cognizant that the Israeli parliament or Knesset has a block of Israeli citizens represented by the Communist Party. One is hard pressed to find a comparable communist party representative entrenched within the infrastructure of an Arab country. As I stated previously, the very nature of the Arab culture and religion would preclude any alliance with communism.

THE P.L.O. AND THE PALESTINIANS

"We Palestinians are buffeted by every wind that blows across the Arab world. If Saudi Arabia and Egypt fall out, we pay the price. If Iraq and Syria are at odds, we are caught in the middle. If Muslim fights Christian in Lebanon, we suffer."

So expressed a top oil consultant in Beirut, Lebanon, who is one of the more than two million Palestinians displaced by the occupation of Palestine. This remark represents the feelings of virtually all the Palestinian Arab exiles living as refugees among Arab countries. Though much verbal support has been voiced in the past by various Arab neighbors, these displaced people often evoke ambivalent feelings if not outright hostility from their Arab hosts. In 1970, hundreds of hapless Palestinians died when King Hussein of Jordan ordered his Bedouin troops to drive the Palestinians from his country. From that epic event came the commemorative "Black September," a phrase used to remind Palestinians of that ignoble operation against them.

In the 1960's the Palestinians were expelled virtually en masse from Saudi Arabia because the Saudi regime feared they might be an ideological "fifth column" for Nasser's socialist revolution. But it must be said that much has changed since these events occurred. Today, King Hussein and the Royal Saudi Family have stood firm in their resolve that the Palestinian People must be recognized as an independent Nation, and that they are entitled to return to their original homeland of Palestine. Both Jordan and Saudi Arabia, as well as the other supporting Arab nations of Syria, Iraq, Libya, have taken a firm stand in complete support of a Palestinian Homeland. This unity has, for the first time, demanded the attention of the United States and the other oil-dependent nations of the free world to be focused on the plight and plea of the displaced Palestinian People.

These displaced Palestinians have become embroiled in the continuing struggle for power between Lebanon's Christian Arab minority and Muslim Arab majority. The Christian Phlange Party is fully backed and supported by the Israeli government which utilizes the Phlange as a buffer against Palestinians now residing in the refugee camps of Lebanon. Daily newspaper and television stories record the death and destruction occurring in the once beautiful country of Lebanon. Even as this book is being written, the destruction of refugee camps and Arab villages bombed and destroyed by Israeli military continues.

Who are the Palestinians? The image of the Palestinian as an illiterate peasant living in a squalid refugee camp, or as a cold-blooded terrorist with assault rifle in hand, is now largely a manufactured myth of the propagandistic media in the western world.

It is true that well over 1.5 million Palestinians still live in the 63 refugee camps in Jordan, Syria, Lebanon and the occupied West Bank and Gaza Strip. But thousands of others who fled their homeland during successive Israeli persecution and the Arab-Israeli wars comprise a sophisticated and well-educated minority. The Palestinians are among the best educated and motivated among the Arab People, and as such, they play a vital role in the political and economic life of much of the Arab world. As teachers, doctors, businessmen, civil servants and technicians, they have found a ready welcome for their know-how and business acumen and have helped spark an economic boom in Saudi Arabia, Kuwait, Qatar and Abu Dhabi. In recognition of their valuable contributions, these Palestinians have been granted special privileges and enjoy positions close to the source of power. In Saudi Arabia, several key positions which surround the Crown Prince are held by Palestinians.

Over the past several years an attitude of schizophrenia was often displayed by many of the so-called "confrontation states" bordering Israel towards the Palestinians. Jordan was once so supportive of the displaced Palestinians that Jordan became a quasi-Palestinian state. Palestinians still outnumber the Bedouins in Jordan. They comprise nearly 70 percent of the population of the capital city of Amman. They own more than 80 percent of the land and businesses in the city. Palestinians can be found at every level of civil service and the upper reaches of the government as well. Jordan is still, as of this writing, the only Arab country that automatically issues passports enabling Palestinians to travel abroad.

In Syria and Egypt, the Palestinians are tolerated and sometimes lauded as heroes of the Arab cause, but they are kept under close surveillance. However, it must be stated that Syria has provided Palestinian commandos with arms, training and logistical support. Yet Syrian police are stationed in Palestinian refugee camps and though most Palestinians enjoy full citizenship status, they are denied Syrian passports.

The Egyptians have grown increasingly irritated by the Palestinians, as they are viewed as "responsible" for being the primary stumbling block to a desired peace with Israel. Peace between Egypt and Israel is a matter for the two nations to determine and implement but not at the expense of the rights and claims of the Palestinians. In other words, is it not absurd to "blame" the Palestinian People for becoming refugees and exiles and therefore, the cause of continued hostility between Egypt and Israel? Should not this blame be reserved for the true antagonist of the dilemma, the Zionist state of Israel? Can one fail to understand why the Palestinians would resist any peace accord between Israel and any Arab nation while their own cause goes unheard and unreconciled?

But I must say that President Sadat of Egypt maintained the necessity of a just settlement of the Palestinian People to be the key to a total and encompassing peace among the Middle East countries. During the historic and courageous visit of Sadat to Israel in 1977, and in his subsequent address to the Knesset he stated:

> "A separate agreement between Egypt and Israel cannot guarantee a just peace. Furthermore, even if peace is achieved between Israel and all the confrontation states, without a just solution of the Palestinian problem, it will not bring that just and stable peace for whose attainment the whole world is pressing."

Lebanon has been nearly destroyed by internal strife between the several factions fighting for power. A major cause of turmoil is the large number of Palestinians living in southern Lebanon who launch military forays into Israel which in turn provoke massive retaliatory shellings and air strikes which are, in most instances, grossly exaggerated responses or overkills.

Lebanese citizens are justifiably irritated by the continuous destruction of both their country and economy. The Palestinians chose southern Lebanon due to its close approximation to the northern Israeli border. Israel continues to funnel military arms and supplies to the Christian Phlange Party who have remained in a grim deadlock with Syrian troops asked to enter the country during one of the numerous civil wars between Muslim and Christian Lebanese. The Phlange oppose the Palestinians as well as the Muslims. Israel has sent its own troops into Lebanese territory whenever it determined their Phlange "allies" were in danger of losing their struggle. Obviously, it is to Israel's advantage to fan the flames and to encourage the continuation of this internal strife between and among Arabs within Lebanon. But once again, the Palestinians are considered the cause of the economical collapse and the extreme Israeli retaliation.

While many of the Palestinians have brought learning, expertise and sophistication with them, they have also carried all the seeds of political and social upheaval that expectedly accompanies an aggrieved and dispossessed people.

The Palestine Liberation Organization (PLO) came into existence in 1964 but did not reach its present size and strength until some major conflicts occurred including the series of "short" wars in 1967, 1972 and 1973, and numerous other conflicts. The men of the PLO are called "fedayeen" meaning "men of sacrifice." The PLO is comprised of eleven guerilla organizations led, in most cases, by individual charismatic men who differ from one another in philosophy but are virtually agreed in their goal of regaining Palestine as their Homeland. Nearly all Palestinians feel they must have the PLO as spokesmen for their grievances. Nabeel Shaath, a Palestinian who lectures in economics at the American University in Beirut, Lebanon:

"Cruel events since '67 have taught us one thing, the only

way to get the world to notice us is to speak and act as Palestinians."

Mohammed Milhem, mayor of Halhoul in occupied West Bank:

"In only ten years the PLO has done more to benefit the people on the West Bank than anyone else."

Perhaps the most extreme guerilla organization is the Popular Front for the Liberation of Palestine (P.F.L.P.). Organized by a Palestine-born Christian physician named George Habash, the PFLP has become the fastest-growing guerilla organization because of the group's well executed and widely publicized raids. Syria has formed its own fedayeen known as Al-Saiqa (the thunderbolt) and Iraq likewise with a small organization known as the Arab Liberation Front (ALF).

In September of 1970 a series of skyjackings occurred, mostly by the PFLP. One of the hostages said, upon release:

"They (Palestinians) think the idea of one nation with one religion is prejudiced, and they were kicked out of their homes. After hearing their side, I think they have some valid points."

Nearly all Palestinian Arabs have given unanimous consent to Yassar Arafat and the PLO to be their representative at any peace conference or discussion of their future and the future of Palestine. Yet Israel and the United States continue to refuse to negotiate or talk with the PLO, claiming they (the PLO) are all terrorists. This point is poorly taken in light of the U.S. government's recent fifteen month negotiation with Iran, who kidnapped and held for ransom, fifty-two American citizens. So it would seem that once again American politicians give forth verbiage pleasing to Israel but without significant truth in demonstration. Perhaps it is now a question of selectivity, in that the terrorist Kholmeni was "approved" and "qualified" for U.S. negotiation, whereas Arafat somehow is "non-acceptable."

All things change with time, and as more and more non-Arab nations are granting the PLO formal diplomatic recognition, the United States must soon decide on its own, for its own welfare, whether to maintain such an inconsistent attitude or accept the inevitable. Initiatives are underway to win United Nations endorsement of a Palestinian state. There are Europen plans to convene new Mideast talks with the PLO sitting in, if U.S. sponsored talks continue to fail.

In the words of Amos Perlmutter, American University Mideast expert:

> *"We should make direct contact and encourage the PLO to make any changes necessary for negotiation, even if not in consultation with Israel."*

Before any semblance of order, let alone peace talks can begin, it is absolutely essential that all principle parties must recognize the PLO is not going to disappear, and must eventually be included in any and all considerations. This is a primary political reality. The PLO continues to grow in strength and worldwide support. They can be temporarily subdued but cannot be eliminated.

More than any of the other Arab peoples, the fedayeen fit the description set forth by T. E. Lawrence in his "Seven Pillars of Wisdom" written more than 40 years ago:

> *"They were as unstable as water, and like water would perhaps finally prevail."*

Will the Palestinians prevail? In one sense they already have, for the world will never again be able to ignore them without attempting to find at least some justifiable solution for their plight.

JEWISH TERRORISTS.....THE OTHER SIDE OF THE COIN

As this book is written, there are numerous reports of continual bombings, beatings and other terrorist activities perpetrated against the Palestinians living in Jerusalem, the West Bank and Gaza Strip. Though rarely reported by the news media with the same intensity and regularity as those events attributed to Arab guerila groups, they nonetheless do occur regularly and have become increasingly violent over the past years of 1977-1982.

During the first two weeks of June, 1980, car bombs were detonated in assassination attempts upon two prominent Arab mayors. Mayor Bassam Shaka'a of Nablus and Mayor Karim Khalaf of Ramallah were both injured seriously. Mayor Shaka'a lost both legs. The attacks had been well coordinated by a team of Israeli terrorists, and not random acts by one or two individual troublemakers. That same day, Mayor Ibrahim Tawil of Bireh, the sister city of Ramallah, narrowly escaped injury from a bomb planted in his garage. The attacks were preceded by detonation of a time bomb planted in the Arab marketplace at Hebron, some 30 miles south of Ramallah. Seven Palestinians were injured in that explosion. These assassination attempts seemed even to shock a segment of the Jewish population of Israel. An organization calling itself "Israeli Freedom Fighters Movement" claimed responsibility for the bombings.

A second radical extremist group called "KACH" (meaning "thus" in Hebrew) was suspected of some involvement. This group was formed by the radical Rabbi Meir Kahane, former head of the Jewish Defense League (JDL). Kahane was arrested and detained by Jerusalem police under an administrative detention order. Kahane vowed, "two teeth for a tooth." Who are these Jewish extremists on the occupied West Bank who are fast bringing the territory to a flash point? Most of them migrated to the 68 settlements that have been illegally established in the West Bank since it was captured by Israel in 1967. Many came because of the belief that they were settling in "Eretz Israel," a term used by Jews to denote the biblical land of the prophets. But most Jewish terrorists are open adherents of political Zionism which advocates expansionism and assimilation of Palestine. Their zealous nationalism spawns increasingly violent confrontations between local Arab inhabitants of the West Bank and the Jewish "new arrivals." It is not uncommon for the nationalists to roam among the Arab districts smashing windows and slashing tires, even invading Arab homes and beating up their occupants. These cowardly and despicable actions are "backed up" by the Israeli military. The nationalists have acquired disproportionate political power and independence within Israel, to the point that even Israeli officials fear an outright insurrection might occur if the government were to "crack down" on their nefarious activities. Most right-wing militant terrorists have some relationship to one of two main groups; the Greater Israel Movement or The Kach. The Greater Israel Movement was formed in 1967 with the aim of annexing the West Bank. The terrorist Rabbi Meir Kahane, a Brooklyn-born American citizen, founded the Kach in Israel in 1974. The "religious" Rabbi admits that less than 30% of his followers are Orthodox Jews. Thus their motivation is not born of "spiritual Jewishness" but rather serves as a classic example of present-day Zionism. Both organizations pay lip service to the propaganda slogan of desiring to govern Israel according to biblical precepts. If their wishes were sincere and were sincerely carried out, then Kahane and Kohorts would be sentenced to death under the Mosaic Law for intentional murder and assorted acts of violence. Kahane openly advocates violence to drive the Arabs out of the West Bank.

A somewhat less extreme militant group is the larger Gush Emunim, meaing "Group of the Faithful." Founded in 1973 by Rabbi Moshe Levinger, Gush urges a policy of aggressive Jewish settlements in all occupied Arab lands. In several instances it has used the tactic of illegal squatting until de facto settlement is finally recognized by the Israeli government. After the bombings previously discussed, Yossi Dayan, a spokesman for Kach said:

> *"We warned these mayors that they had to leave Eretz Israel. If they had listened to us, they would be able to walk today."*

It is a political reality that both Arab and Jew have active terrorist groups and organizations; both have inflicted terror and tragedy upon a civilian population. Innocent women and children, Arab and Jew, have been maimed and killed as a direct result of terrorist actions. The Arabs attempt to intimidate those they see as enemies occupying their homes and country; they try to attract the attention of the world to their displacement. The Jews react to terror with anti-terror activities and utilize every opportunity to drive the Arabs from their own, legally owned homes and lands in the name of nationalism. Palestinians are convinced that only violence and bloodshed can drive the Israelis from occupied Arab land. Israelis are just as convinced they have a God-given right to the West Bank and nothing, and no one, can force them to leave.

ILLEGAL SETTLEMENTS AND LAND GRABBING

The absolute most offensive activity conducted by the present government and the Jewish people against the native Arab inhabitants is the taking over of Arab homes, lands and possessions. After the 1967 War, Israel's Labor Party then in power, allowed Jewish settlers to live in the Jordan Valley, primarily on the ridge above the valley. These settlements were considered as a defensive line between Jordan and Israel's heavily populated coastal areas. Yet they were well removed from the Arab population in general, and were not especially criticized by the Arabs. When in 1977 Menachen Begin's Likud coalition assumed power, Jewish settlements began immediately sprouting up throughout the West Bank. As of June 1980, it was estimated there were at least 68 settlements totalling about 14,000 Jewish residents on the West Bank outside of East Jerusalem. In January of 1981 it was announced that Mr. Begin planned to sponsor another EIGHTEEN SETTLEMENTS and to "plant" some 13,000 Jews in what has been up to now, completely Arab owned and Arab occupied land.

These settlements, contrary to the loud claims of the Israeli government, have very little military or economic value. Their true value is one of propaganda in that they serve as a highly visible demonstration of Israel's claim to the land. The world nations, including the United States, collectively oppose any and all settlements and view them as illegal and primary obstacles to a Mideast peace. The Israelis seem divided on the issue. A 1980 poll split 50-50 on the need to establish new settlements. Former President Carter considered the settlements to be a violation of international law and an obstacle in achieving a lasting peace. One U.S. State Department official said:

"Begin has gone too far, not once, but several times. The

situation in the West Bank is dynamite, and no one over there is acting to defuse it."

A growing number of Jewish leaders are beginning to call for a halt to any continued new settlements or expansion. Begin's continued intransigence on the question of Palestinian autonomy, and his coddling of the extremist Jewish settlers and their supporters, places great responsibility upon him as a direct contributor to the climate of violence. The Jerusalem Post said of the bombings in the week of June 9, 1980:

"They were a process whose roots lie in the concept of perpetual Jewish rule in the West Bank, but whose shoots are the denial of coexistence."

Not all Israeli government leaders agree with this policy. Many have in the past and are even now openly expressing their opposition to the expansionistic, belligerent attitude of the current leaders. The late General Moyshe Dayan and former Defense Minister Ezer Weizman, two of the most popular and well-known Israeli citizen-soldiers, have both resigned.

Begin has defied the United States, Egypt, and in fact nearly all the nations of the world in promoting the establishment of new settlements in occupied West Bank. He insists that Jews must be free to settle anywhere they wish in historic Palestine, regardless of the fact that the desired land chosen for settlement is already owned and occupied by native Palestinian Arabs.

EAST JERUSALEM TOO?

As if more fuel were needed for the fires of hatred and mistrust between Arab and Jew, Mr. Begin's government announced in 1980 their decision to "annex" the city of Jerusalem, moving their capital from Tel Aviv to Jerusalem. Thus we encounter the most intractable problem of all, for the Arab half of the city annexed by Israel after its victory in the 1967 War is being claimed as part and parcel of the Jewish capital. Palestinians make it clear that they consider East Jerusalem's 100,000 Arabs to be residents of the West Bank, not Israel. They insist that East Jerusalem Arabs should vote in any elections held. Every Israeli government since 1967 has vowed never to give up the control of the city. To prove their determination, more than 50,000 Jews have been settled in new suburbs east of the city where virtually none lived before 1967. A 10,000 unit apartment complex has been completed as part of a circle of Jewish civilian enclaves surrounding Jerusalem. A second circle of encampments further north is nearly complete.

The Israeli electorate is beginning to make itself heard. A recent poll of Jewish voters found that almost half opposed the building of any more Israeli settlements on Arab land, compared with only 35 percent who approved. A major reason for the opposition within Israel is the burden of governing the 825,000 Palestinians on the West Bank and the 400,000 in the Gaza Strip. Added to this is their reluctance to meet the cost of new settlements during Israel's period of 160 percent inflation. Beyond these reasons, however, a growing number of Israelis view the military occupation of Arab land as morally offensive.

Presently, the settlers have no legal claim to the lands they have taken even under Israeli law. It has been "requisitioned" from its Arab owners by the Israeli government for "state purposes." The settlers are demanding the Knesset pass a law giving them legal title.

The only parties who really stand to gain from the current crisis are not the Jewish and Arab populations. The PLO needs continued violence to motivate greater resistance, and the JDL and Gush Emunim exploit the violence to press for even greater Israeli domination over the occupied West Bank and Gaza Strip. Even a staunch supporter of settlement policies as Ehud Olmert, a member of the Knesset cautioned:

"There is a growing sense that things are going too far. Some feel what happens corrupts Israel as a moral and democratic society."

Settlement mentality has become the proverbial back-breaking straw of the Palestinian Camel. Bloodshed intensifies and potential peace draws further away. Jewish settlers on the West Bank, who as of June 16, 1980, comprised a mere

2% of the population excluding Jerusalem, have stepped up their demands for support of their take-over policy. When followers of Rabbi Moshe Levinger illegally attempted to re-establish a Jewish presence in the Arab city of Hebron after an absence of more than 40 years, the Begin government allowed them to remain. The result was a Jewish student killed by a sniper bullet. In reprisal, the Israeli government approved the building of two religious schools in Hebron's former Jewish quarter long since totally occupied by Arabs. These decisions led directly to even more violence as six Jews were killed outside the Haddassah clinic in Hebron. These are the events which preceded the bombings of the three Arab Mayors related earlier.

Perhaps it will be the youthful future leaders of both sides who will finally begin to express the truth of this involved situation and who will then begin the process of retribution and restoration.

An amazing occurrence was reported in the world press on April 10, 1981. Gadi Elgazi, a 19-year old private in the Israeli army was imprisoned by his superiors for refusing to join his tank unit in the occupied West Bank of the Jordan River. During his military trial, he cited his opposition to the exiling of local Arabs, the demolition of houses suspected of harboring terrorists, and the shooting of student rioters. Elgazi belongs to a growing organization of young Israelis called "Group 27." Contained in their manifesto is the following:

"We reject an occupation that turns our people into oppressors and the Palestinians into the oppressed. Service in the captured areas goes against our consciences and political convictions."

The situation will worsen. More and more Arabs support the PLO and its call for a solution by force. Palestinians are becoming so desperate and radicalized that moderation is nearly disappearing from the thinking of West Bank residents. More and more strikes, demonstrations, confrontations and death are bound to increase.

Chapter 5

BIBLICAL PROPHECY AND
THE PROMISED LAND

THE CLAIM IS made by the current leaders (Zionist) of Israel and many of their supporters that the occupation and expansion of Jewish settlements on Arab land is the mere fulfillment of Biblical prophecy which promised them (the Jews) the land of Palestine forever. We will examine the primary biblical texts or prophecies most often cited to justify the occupation of Palestine. Each major "proof-text" will be examined in the light of biblical context, historical contemporaneity, with the application of basic rules of interpretation.

Before any reader of any work of literature can ascertain the import and meaning intended by the author, he must first be aware of the required rules which, when known and applied, will prevent the reader from drawing invalid conclusions. The rules we will briefly consider comprise the science of interpretation called "Hermeneutics" which comes from the Greek word "Hermeneutikos" meaning "to interpret." The literal meaning is the study of the methodological principles of interpretation.

Hermeneutics is the science of interpretation, and Exegesis is the practical application of the rules or principles of this science in determining the intended message of the author. These simple principles find their justification in the dictates of common sense.

As mathematic conclusions can derive no force or meaning from the authority of mathematicians, and since all that is truly scientific is independent of any such authority, the results of careful exegesis of any book conducted under the faithful application of the laws of hermeneutics must be received without reference to any supposed authority of exegetes. In other words, the authority in any work of literature is the source under examination, rather than the examiner or reader.

An "authoritative" expositor or reader is as needless as an authoritative chemist, except in the case of inspired revelation of what had been previously only partially revealed. The Old Testament Scriptures of the Bible were in need of such special exposition, and the Old Testament Prophets perfectly fulfilled that need. Likewise the Apostles of Christ were especially endowed by God with the ability to interpret and apply the Messianic prophecies to the life, work and teachings of Jesus Christ. But this requirement and need for special expositors of the Biblical text has come and gone with the Prophets and the Apostles, and no such need exists for today's world. But the use of hermeneutical rule will aid every reader to arrive at the same conclusion and understanding of an author's intended meaning.

Hermeneutics as a science, embracing fixed principles founded on common sense, effactually excludes all claims to the office of authoritative or infallible interpretation for mankind. The authority has always remained with the original text and not the reader.

Using hermeneutics, no one is free to claim a "private interpretation" nor a license to pursue their own personal views or persuasions when reading a book. No one is free from the control or wholesome guidance of specific laws that do not vary. All have the liberty to follow this scientific leading to legitimate results apart from dogmatic dictation from any source.

Often, men will claim that an authoritative standard or understanding of a particular book must be established to prevent unlimited variation or wild, extravagant interpretation by others reading the same book. Both these statements are based upon the false assumption that there is no science of hermeneutics. As a science with laws to be strictly obeyed and observed in interpretation, hermeneutics stands equally opposed to authoritative dictation on one hand, and to lawless interpretation or exegesis on the other.

God, the Author of revealed truth, indisputably intending to be understood, has so fully and clearly set forth the meaning to be understood for the benefit of mankind, that nothing short of a false exegesis involving the neglect or deliberate repudiation of the principles of heremeneutics can obscure the true sense and meaning of the Divine Word. Simply stated, there can be no difference of opinion as to the meaning of biblical texts if every reader will practice a few basic hermeneutical rules of interpretation. As one confronts the myriad of books flooding the market, especially those "Prophecy" or "Last Days" booklets found in nearly every Christian Book Store and in many personal libraries of Evangelical ministers, it is ever apparent that the multitude of authors are totally unaware of the hermeneutical rules and thusly, their readers are believing and receiving distorted, bias interpretations which amount to nothing more than the doctrinal persuasion of the denominational writer.

Biblical Hermeneutics brings the earnest and objective reader to a position on which the light of Divine truth is allowed to fall in all the fullness and clarity of its own teaching. The biblical testimony on any subject, whether given in one locus or several, must be taken in its entirety without abridgement or modification so that the scriptures may interpret themselves in the broad clear light of their divine teaching

The laws of interpretation are certain sensible directions to be followed as indispensable for bringing the learning mind of man into uninterrupted contact with the instructing mind of God.

SUBJECTIVE CONDITIONS

It is vital that one interpreting the scriptures be fully conversant with the hermeneutical rules of literature and be in a truly open and nonpartisan or prejudicial state of mind.

Freedom from bias is absolutely indispensable.

Hermeneutical freedom is, in the first place, freedom from all intellectual presuppositions. It is, in the second place, freedom from every moral bias such as the lack of candor or sincerity. Any writer or interpreter of literature must be free from the dogmatism of others as well as exempt from the dogmatism of his own.

These mental qualifications of the reader or interpreter are also referred to as the subjective conditions of reliable exegesis. They deserve added emphasis in this chapter, for it is precisely the lack of such mental qualifications which has produced, in my opinion, the gross interpretations of the scriptures now being held by many conservative, evangelical churches which support the state of Israel in occupied Palestine. A very few "authors" and their non-hermeneutical interpretations of Old Testament Scriptures are responsible for many well-meaning Christians aligning themselves with Zionism and its adherents, and against the truly aggrieved and maligned Palestinian Arab People.

For anyone to determine biblical teachings, one must possess the discriminating ability, analytical power, and logical acumen obtained by application and understanding of Biblical Hermeneutics. One must be able to distinguish between the ideas embodied in expressions that may closely resemble each other in form yet differ essentially in significance. A sentence may appear as another, but its real meaning is determined by its usage.

Any interpreter or author who, applying faithfully the principles of hermeneutics in full possession of intellectual freedom and sincerity with himself and his God, will find the biblical word to be intelligible and revealing.

It would seem apparent that a major requisite for anyone desiring to interpret the biblical text or author a biblical book should be capable of reading the Bible in the original languages in which it was written, Hebrew and Greek. Many so-called "contradictions" and apparent discrepancies, as well as far-out eschatological theories which border on irrationality, disappear. Yet it seems the majority of popular "prophecy" books selling today are written by men or women who cannot read or understand either language.

The Bible is a book written to be understood. Its authors never intended its message to be "mysterious" or "hidden" from mankind. It is addressed to all men and can be understood by all men. The Revelation of God must never be considered "too hard" to understand, thereby necessitating an "authority" or self-proclaimed modern-day prophet who has a special "gift" to interpret the text. The meaning of the biblical text is not "up for grabs" and cannot be honestly wrenched and dissected to support man-made, outlandish teachings. Proper interpretation is to allow the original writer of the text to express his original and intended meaning, and to accept that meaning as final! To this end the rest of this chapter is written.

BIBLICAL PROPHECY EXAMINED

As we study the prophecies contained within the Older Testament we will note any parallel passages relative to the topic at hand. Perhaps the single most common reason for the majority of misinterpretations and outlandish teachings as to biblical prophecy and Israel is the failure to interpret every passage and expression IN THE LIGHT OF THE CONTEXT, OR CONNECTION WITH CONTIGUOUS STATEMENTS! Any exposition or rendering given without regard to context is unsafe; and any exposition or rendering given in direct conflict with the context is most assuredly unsafe and untrue.

No passage can be understood apart from the HISTORICAL CIRCUMSTANCES connected with its composition. This is another of the "keys" we will use to unlock the massive maze of false interpretations of biblical prophecy. It is absolutely vital that we be aware of contemporary history and all archaeological findings before concluding whether a biblical prophecy was, is, or shall be fulfilled.

A classic example of the application of hermeneutical rules to the biblical text is in the reading of the Parables given by Jesus Christ in Matthew 13, Mark 4 and Luke 8. In each instance Christ *HIMSELF* gives first the parable, and then the explanation as to meaning of His parables. Christ is the original author, and His own explanation is sufficient and final. Yet today one will find numerous books on the Parables of Christ with outlandish, subjective interpretations which utterly fail in ascertaining the simple and truthful intent of the parables as stated by Christ himself. This unjustified "bending" of the text is rarely questioned by church members or even their pastors. If you will re-read the preceding pages of this chapter you will see how this type of scripture "twisting" cannot occur if one follows the rules of hermeneutics. You can also understand the need for all Christians to be aware of this science.

There are four cardinal points of all literature:

(a) Description...the incident itself belongs to the past, the words describing it are throughout the words of the author himself. Good examples are Homer and Milton.

(b) Presentation...the author himself nowhere appears but he leaves the reader to hear words of those personages who actually took part in the incident, perhaps to see their own doings. Good examples are Shakespeare and Bacon.

(c) Poetry..."Creative literature," the poet makes something or he creates or adds to the sum of existence by figures, symbols and other poetic vehicles. Example, Bunyon.

(d) Prose...only discusses what already exists, such as an allegory, imaginative from God.

The most important distinguishing feature of Hebrew literature is its overlapping of prose with poetry. Prophecy in one of its aspects may be described as the philosophy of history erected into a drama. This is called a "rhapsody." The Bible is filled with literary devices. It has simile and metaphor and a host of other nonliteral expressions which have to be understood before a particular verse or teaching can make proper sense. The Old Testament writers use litotes (understatement) and hyperbole (overstatement), anthropomorphism (ascription of human form and feeling to God) and anthropopathy (feeling to Spirit). It uses oxymoron and irony, personification and satire and many more. The point is, if one writes irony and the reader fails to interpret ironically, a completely opposite point may be made from that intended.

A special need exists for all Christians and bible readers, and that need is awareness of how the bible is written, and an understanding of figurative language as employed by the biblical writers. I am going to list some of the principle figures of speech found in the Bible. Remember, a figure of speech is the extension of a word or expression beyond its ordinary acceptation for the sake of ornament or emphasis.

(1) Metaphor...a figure which applies the name of one thing to another because of some resemblance, real or supposed, between them. A good example, "You are a temple of God."

(2) Simile...a figure which indicates resemblance by a formal comparison using such terms as "like," "as," etc. Example, "All flesh is as grass, and all the glory as the flower of grass."

(3) Allegory...a figure based upon resemblance and indirectly suggests one thing through the representation of another. In Psalm 80:8-14 Israel is allegorically represented by a vine.

(4) Metonomy...exchanges the name of one thing for that of another due to some relation between them. Romans 8:10, "The Spirit is life because of righteousness." An abstract term used for reality.

(5) Antithesis...grouping of opposites in a formal contrast. Romans 6:23, "The wages of sin is death, but the gift of God is eternal life."

(6) Paradox...opposites seem affirmed of one and the same subject. As in Matthew 10:39, "He that finds his life shall lose it."

(7) Irony...when what is meant is the opposite of what is asserted. Job 12:2, "No doubt you are the people, and all wisdom shall die with you."

(8) Hyperbole...an exaggeration for the purpose of expressing the full force of the subject. Psalm 119:136, "Rivers of waters run down my eyes, because they keep not your law."

(9) Allusion...a truth is indirectly designated by ironical application of a term used falsely by others as descriptive of the subject. I Corinthians 1:21, "It was God's good pleasure through the foolishness of preaching to save those who believe."

(10) Personification...inanimate objects clothed with attributes of animate. Isaiah 55:1, "All trees of the field will clap their hands."

(11) Paronomasia...a play on words and a figure in which a word is repeated with a variation in the sense. Matthew 8:2, "Follow me; and let the dead bury their dead."

(12) Interrogation...asking of a question not for information but to make a strong affirmation or denial. Romans 8:33, "Who shall bring a charge against God's chosen ones?"

(13) Anthropomorphism...ascribes human features and feelings to God. I Peter 3:12, "The Lord's eyes are directed in a favourable attitude towards the righteous, and His ears are inclined to their petitions, but His face is against those who practice evil things."

(14) Anthropopathy...ascribes human affections to God. Genesis 6:6, "And the Lord was sorry He had made men on earth, and He was grieved in His heart."

(15) Climax...arranging the thought in gradual levels of increase, rising from a lower to a higher concept. I Corinthians 12:28, "And God indeed placed some for His own use in the Church, first apostles; second, prophets; third, teachers; then workers of miracles; then gifts of healing; also those whose ministry it is to help others; and administrators; and different languages." This is an example of the reverse, falling importance from the higher to the lower which is languages.

Now once a familiarity with these basic figurative expressions is mastered, the interpreter or exegete must demonstrate his common sense and intelligence by carefully distinguishing between a figurative word and a figurative thing, not looking for a representative object where a mere figure of speech occurs, and vice versa. When Paul says of the rock from which the Israelites drank that, "The rock was Christ" he uses no figure of speech but pointed to a representative object as a type of Him who is the blessed source of "living water." (I Corinthians 10:4)

Of vital importance is the law for legitimate distinction between the literal and figurative. We can regard neither a word nor a thing as figurative unless it would be absurd or unreasonable to do otherwise. Wild and fanciful interpretation, especially in Prophecy, abound in the popular writings of today. To these writers, the entire Bible is full of horrible scenes of death, miraculous physical occurrences such as mountains actually "growing" so they can "fit" their end-times predictions, etc. When Jesus said, "I am the true vine, and my Father is the vinedresser," He obviously uses figurative language and anyone who would take this as a literal teaching would be declared a fool. (John 15:1)

This failure to distinguish between literal and figurative lies at the very heart of the faulty interpretations believed and taught by many including the Final return of Christ, the Kingdom of God, and the imagined "return of the Jews to Israel." It is this type of credulity which perhaps can explain how any rational Christian can ever imagine that God could support the total injustice and dishonest actions taken by any nation or group of people towards another. Making all scriptures and prophecies "literal" and futuristic, the "text benders" can place the blame for deception, blatant lies and evil scheming on an unparalleled level, all upon God and His Word.

I have not intended to conduct a class in Hermeneutical principles or the Laws of Interpretation. However, from the cursory introduction we have just concluded, it is hoped that the reader can appreciate the importance of hermeneutics and will attempt to apply these principles as you continue reading this book as well as other literature. At the conclusion of this chapter, you will find a number of references and sources for the continued study of Hermeneutics and Prophecy in the reading list and Bibliography.

DOES ISRAEL HAVE A BIBLICAL BASIS
FOR CLAIMING PALESTINE TODAY?

To some this question may seem irrelevant, but to those deeply concerned about the mideast conflict it is a vital issue involving Biblical interpretation. The re-establishment of Israel as a political state in Palestine has focused the attention of Bible readers upon the future of Israel and the significance of the original promise to Abraham of the possession of Canaan. Does this land really belong to Israel by "divine right"? To answer the question, I propose to present the issue as it is represented in the biblical text. In the biblical text there are four distinct segments comprising the Promises made to Abraham and his seed. If these four questions or segments are answered properly in an honest attitude, we will emerge with agreement as to whether the present-day Israeli occupation is within the providence of "God's Will."

The four questions or segments we must consider are:

(1) What was the land promise God made to Abraham?

(2) Is the "Larger Land of Canaan" promise the same as the promise of land to Israel?

(3) Did God intend for Abraham, Isaac, and Jacob to inherit that land personally?

(4) Was the land promise fulfilled, or only in part, and today's land seizure by Israel is the second and final part of original prophecy?

It will not be my intention to consider and refute the many confusing and contradictory teachings such as Premillenialism, the supposed "rapture" of the Church, the "tribulation," or the terrible "end times" ideas which include a physical, literal battle called "Armagheddon." I am preparing a book which will deal specifically with these popular but incorrect teachings currently promulgated by various churches.

WHY SO MUCH INTEREST IN PROPHECY?

Before we continue our in-depth examination of prophecy, I

deem it important to address this question. There is far too much emphasis and interest in what is incorrectly termed "prophecy" which is, in reality, something called eschatology, which is a doctrine of the last or final things some imagine are contained within the scriptures. Perhaps this "obsession" with the future is directly related to the many potential world explosions and international confrontations which seems to have produced an assemblage of "believers" who are heaping to themselves expositers who dwell on what they consider to be the final events to occur with the Consummation of the Ages, the return of Jesus Christ.

I am concerned with what has fast become a preoccupation of many with projected eschatological events, the fascination born out of a basis of fear and fright, turmoil and anxiety. I am concerned that the popular emphasis in the study of prophecy is such as to INCREASE rather than to allay this fear and anxiety. Christian Book stores, radio and television are filled with preachers and self-proclaimed prophets who seem to delight in playing on the fears and anxieties of people. In fact, many magnify the threat to peace and say little of the "things that make for peace." These "prophets" are much too concerned to identify men, nations, and daily events in terms of some specific biblical prophecy.

They focus attention on "antichrists" rather than on Christ; they seem more concerned to prove what prophecy says about Russia, China, or "Gog" and "Magog," Israel and Great Britain, rather than to proclaim what the Bible teaches about the Kingdom of God in the lives of men and women. This obsession has led men to predict time and time again both the end of the material world and the second advent of Jesus Christ, and time and time again they have been wrong. Their nonbiblical, near illiterate predictions have reinforced the scorn, derision and skepticism of an unbelieving world towards the entire Revelation of God.

Undaunted by failure, they continue to roll out the books prophesying doom and gloom, invasions by communist countries, etc. All the while failing to fortify and edify hungry Christians in need of biblical knowledge for daily growth and spiritual maturity. The prophetic pied-pipers may lead to the "end of the world" hysteria as they presumptiously claim to predict and interpret "times and seasons" which "the Father has fixed by His own authority." (Acts 1:7) It is of little consequence that Christ Himself said, of his own return, "of that day and hour no one knows, not even the angels of heaven, or the Son, but the Father only." (Matthew 24:36) This audacious attitude is carried over into their interpretation of biblical prophecy. This wrong use of prophecy carries within itself a faulty exegesis. The emphasis is wrong because attention is focused primarily on the transient events instead of the redemptive activity of the living God.

The exegesis is wrong because it does not understand the fundamental nature and purpose of prophecy, and ignores basic evangelical, hermeneutical principles used for interpretation of literature. This wrong use of prophecy can never give to the human heart the faith, hope and love that casts out fear. Thus, those who listen to these exponents of gloom, death and tribulation, are easy prey for the books and programs claiming to contain the details of our future, and within this context, the events currently comprising the Palestinian Conflict between the Zionist Israeli military government and the Palestinian Arabs.

HISTORICAL CONTEMPORANEITY

The first significance of prophecy is as a message for the Prophet's own day and time. As one reads the writings of any prophet, we *must* assume the stated prophecy was given in his own day to his own people unless it is stated otherwise, elsewhere in the biblical record. Many of today's expositors who force the scriptures to support Israel seem to be unaware of three important ideas involved in this interpretative principle:

(1) The function of the prophet was first of all that of a teacher and a preacher. The Hebrew use of the term Prophet includes "nabi" which means to speak as God's ambassador. This, of course, does not rule out the element of future prediction. It simply puts the primary emphasis where it belongs: on the prophetic message of repentance, faith and obedience; on the preaching concerning God and man and

the covenant relationship between them; on the teaching concerning sin, judgment, reconciliation and salvation.

(2) The message of the prophet reflects and reveals something of an historical situation to which it is directed. It clothes itself, as Edward Riehm has said so well, in "local color" or "times coloring." The prophetic preaching was effective because it spoke to a definite life situation and is worded in terms of that situation. Again, prophetic statements were not, and are not today, meaningful only in light of forced interpretation of current events and individuals. A small portion of prophetic statements may go beyond historical circumstances of the time and culture in which they were given, BUT OUR FIRST TASK IN INTERPRETATION IS TO ASCERTAIN WHAT IT MEANT FOR THE FAITH, HOPE, AND RELIGIOUS LIVES OF THOSE WHO LIVED WITHIN THAT HISTORICAL SITUATION, AND TO WHOM THE PROPHET WAS SENT AS A SPOKESMAN OF GOD.

First and foremost for any expositor is the consideration of the current events, the historical perspective and background in which a prophecy was given. If these important areas are considered, studied, and applied to exegesis, it will quickly settle nearly all disputes over fulfilled prophecy, and in the course of doing so will firmly put an end to vain speculatory interpretations so popular today.

(3) If a particular text or prophecy does indicate a futuristic interpretation, that interpretation must be considered within the framework of a religious message relevant for the day and the situation in which the prophecy was given or stated.

Without fear of contradiction, I believe that by far, the majority of prophecies recorded in the Old Testament have already been fulfilled. Their fulfillment can be verified by the biblical text and a study of contemporary biblical history. Now if it be true that the prophets, both Minor and Major, spoke in their day to their own people concerning events and attitudes which would directly affect them, NO ONE HAS THE RIGHT TO PROJECT BEYOND THE SITUATION VISUALIZED BY THE PROPHET HIMSELF.

The hermeneutical atrocity of abscribing various prophecies to be disjointed parts of an eschatological picture puzzle to be assembled later without regard to historical origin and cultural realities, is causing multitudes of sincere believers to miss entirely the prophetic message and teaching of the Absolutism of God. Though sincere, they are "sincerely wrong" in adopting the superficial position of end-time literalistic interpretational attitudes towards Biblical Prophecy.

Historical Contemporaneity is more evident in the writings of some prophets than in others. An example is the book of Jeremiah, and the first half of the book of Ezekiel. The prophecy is inextricably entwined with the various events leading up to and culminating in the Chaldean conquest, the fall of Jerusalem in 537-586 B.C., and the beginning of the Babylonian Captivity. The many prophecies given by both men were completely fulfilled through historical events now verifiable in both secular and biblical history. As we continue our study, I deem it wise that all should begin with the working hypothesis that the first significance of any prophecy is as a message for the prophet's own day.

COVENANT BACKGROUND

We have already listed the four major questions or segments which comprise the biblical prophecies of the "Promised Land" given by God to Abraham. Each of these segments, and the primary statements and promises, are all part of the "covenant" of God with all men for all time. Webster's New Collegiate Dictionary defines covenant as "a formal and binding, solemn agreement; a pledge; to enter into a contract."

In the Scriptures it is said that God entered into a "covenant" with Noah and Abraham, Israel and David. These are not separate covenants, but are singularly one covenant; God's redemptive intercession in the history of mankind for the purpose of reconciliation, regeneration, and salvation. It is important we understand this covenant relationship is the framework for the Israelite understanding both of theology and of history. An undeniable direct and fundamental relationship exists between the covenant and prophecy. It follows that a correct understanding of the covenant will help us to correctly interpret prophecy, for every prophecy must be seen within the setting of the covenant promise and hope.

Prophecy must be studied against the background of the covenant of blessing with Abraham, which through Moses became the national covenant with God's people Israel, and then through Jesus Christ found fulfillment in a universal covenant.

If we see nothing more in the covenant with Abraham and Israel than the promise of a seed and a physical land and material inheritance and blessing, then we will have failed to comprehend the real spiritual nature of the message of the prophets. The prophets were concerned with *SPIRITUAL TRUTHS* far more than a "physical nation" or land. Their interpretation of their own situation was primarily *religious* rather than *political.* Yet today we find the complete reverse emphasis which has resulted in misguided Christians supporting the unlawful occupation of Palestine.

The fundamentals of the covenant belong to God's activity and relevation in the past. The prophetic message, whether speaking of sin, judgment, salvation, hope, love, religion, ethics or history, past, present or future, that prophetic message is inseparable from the basic faith of Israel in a God of the covenant. Subsequently, every prophecy must be interpreted in relation to this covenant established by a loving God with all mankind. For an excellent, in-depth study of God's covenant with man, I suggest the book by Jakob Jocz entitled, "The Covenant: A Theology of Human Destiny." (see bibliography.)

PROMISES AND PROPHECIES CONCERNING ISRAEL AND THE LAND OF PALESTINE

The re-establishment of Israel as a political state in the land of Palestine has naturally focused the attention of Bible readers upon the future of present-day Israel and the significance of the land promise originally given to Abraham and his descendants. Our discussion on this and other points will be limited to a basis of three words, "a Biblical basis." What we examine together will be the biblical text and not a host of commentators or eminent theologians and their personal views or expressions as to the prophecies under discussion.

As I once told my students in the college classroom, "The Bible can shed an amazing amount of light on biblical commentaries."

We have already considered many aspects of the Palestinian conflict, a conflict so filled and charged with emotional sympathies and ethical considerations that King Solomon would be hard pressed to render a just and fair solution acceptable to all parties.

Now we shall contemplate the biblical prophecies which form, for the Christian world, an integral part of the conflict. As in our previous chapters, we will review this section from an objective and rational perspective.

(1) First, the land covenant with Abraham and subsequently the land covenant as applied to all Israel.

> *"Now the Lord said to Abraham, Go forth from your country, And from your relatives and from your Father's house, To the land which I will show you; And I will make you a great nation, And I will bless you, and make your name great; And so you shall be a blessing; And I will bless those who bless you, And the one who curses you I will curse. And in you all the families of the earth shall be blessed." (Genesis 12:1-3)*

Within this statement of divine purpose are four elements. Each element is repeated and reaffirmed and clarified as we move through the book of Genesis, the Old Testament, and through the New Testament. Each element is related to Abraham's vocation and to the covenant God made with him.

Abraham is commanded to leave his country and relatives in order to place himself in a position to carry out God's purpose and calling. The first thing we notice is there is more meaning in this first element than simply the physical exodus and geographical considerations. For even this physical move was a religious exercise which involved faith and obedience. We learn that from the very beginning of this covenant, there is a conditional relationship.

Abraham is told to leave, and when he does what he is told, only then will God bless him as He has promised. As we continue to expand our understanding of the land covenant we come to the first element of that promise which will help us understand the total prophecy.

THE SEED PROMISE OR COVENANT

The first element we will call the "seed" promise. The Hebrew word for seed is 'zera' and is a singular-collective noun, which can mean either an individual or descendants, in the sense of a family or nation. The word zera or seed is not actually found in the Genesis text until chapter twelve, verse seven, but God does here state "I will make of you a great nation." This seed promise is attached in Genesis 21:12 to Isaac, "for through Isaac your descendants shall be named," or "in Isaac shall your seed be called." In Isaiah 41:8 the seed is attached to Israel as a nation, "But you, Israel, my servant, Jacob whom I have chosen, desccendant of Abraham my friend." In the New Testament, this seed promise is clearly attached to Jesus Christ, as in Galatians 3:16:

"Now the promises were spoken to Abraham and to his seed, He does not say, 'And to Seeds,' as referring to many, but rather to one, "And to your seed," that is, Christ."

In Galatians 3:29 the attachment is made to every believer:

"And if you belong to Christ, then you are Abrahams offspring, heirs according to promise."

If the seed covenant or promise was meant only for the physical nation of Israel which came out of Egypt, then God's promise was a failure, for the entire world was not necessarily "blessed" by the Jews of 1400 B.C. anymore than by the Egyptians, Assyrians or the Babylonians.

As a nation and people, they were not great builders, architects or warriors. In fact, physical Israel left the world with little more than ancient manuscripts recording their special relationship with the one supreme God and His varied guidance given to them through the Old Testament Prophets. The entire world was blessed, and continues to be blessed, however, through the prophesied cominng of the Messiah (Hebrew "Mashiach"), the Deliverer who reconciled all men to God and to Himself. The Biblical teaching of the seed promise then, is singularly to Christ and those who accept Him as the promised, prophesied Messiah.

THE LAND PROMISE

Our second element is the promise of a physical land, implied in Genesis 12:1 in the command to go, "to the land that I will show you," and in verse two, in that a great nation must necessarily have a land in which to live, and made specific in verse seven, "To your descendants I will give this land."

Many writers emphasize that the land promise is mentioned even more frequently than the deliverance from Egyptian bondage or the promise of the Messiah. But even if this be true, does mere repetition of a statement become the criteria for determining emphasis? The fact is that the land promise is mentioned often but does not become the single most important element in the covenant with Abraham. The central message of all the prophets was the coming of the Messiah. Are we to understand that God is more interested in the physical than the spiritual; the tangibles rather than the intangibles; a single nation as opposed to the welfare of an entire world? Such circumscription of God is borne of limited knowledge and understanding of God and the Bible. This attitude is especially offensive to the plain scriptural teachings as to the character, nature, and expressed desires of an omnipotent God. Careful examination of Genesis 12 reveals that the promise of the land does not stand in the climactic position for that position is reserved for the promise of blessing. The truth is that in the nearly four thousand years from the call of Abraham until now, the seed of Abraham has not even occupied the promised land, much less controlled it for as much as half the time. Not even Abraham, to whom the promise was given, nor Isaac, nor Jacob, "heirs with him of the same promise" (Hebrews 11:9) took the land grant promise as seriously as modern interpreters.

If we apply the rules of hermeneutics to existing scriptures, and we then follow or trace the reaffirmations of this promise of a land through the Old and New Testaments, we begin to see that it is more and more a symbol of something greater, something far beyond physical earth or property. Without manipulation of the text, a serious reader will observe that the land covenant was from the beginning, pointing to a spiritual land or Kingdom. When Christ stood before Pilate and was asked about being a King, Jesus said in John 18:36:

My Kingdom is not of this world. If my Kingdom were of this world, then My servants would be fighting, that I might not be delivered up to the Jews; but as it, My Kingdom is not of this realm."

An example of how one biblical writer interpreted this land promise is recorded by the author of the book of Hebrews, written to Jewish Christians in Rome as an encouragement to retain their faith in Jesus Christ as the Messiah. In Hebrews 11:13-16:

"All these died in faith, without receiving the promises, but having seen them and welcomed them from a distance, and having confessed that they were strangers and exiles on the earth. For those who say such things make it clear that they are seeking a country of their own. And indeed if they had been thinking of that country from which they went out, they would have had opportunity to return. But as it is, they desire a better country, that is a HEAVENLY ONE. Therefore God is not ashamed to be called their God; for He has prepared a city for them."

This Chapter (11) is called the "Faith" chapter. But note carefully that in the preceding verses (4-12) as the writer traces the origin of mankind and the rather sordid occurrences such as Cain slaying his brother Abel, he includes the calling of Abraham and his obedience in following the instructions of God, and yet he brings all the emphasis collectively together in verses 13-16 by saying, "All these died in faith, WITHOUT RECEIVING THE PROMISES, BUT HAVING SEEN THEM AND WELCOMED THEM FROM A DISTANCE." So the land promise was ALWAYS a spiritual promise and was so understood by the early Christian writers.

The "city" referred to in Heb 11:16 is not the earthly, physical city of Jerusalem as many would have us believe. Rather, it too is a spiritual city as clearly indicated in Hebrews 12:18-20, 22-24:

"For you have not come to a mountain that may be touched and to a blazing fire, and to darkness and gloom

*and whirlwind, and to the blast of a trumpet and the
sound of words which sound was such that those who
heard begged that no further word should be spoken to
them. But you have come to Mount Zion and to the city
of the living God, the HEAVENLY JERUSALEM, and to
myriads of angels, to the general assembly and church of
the first-born who are all enrolled in heaven, and to God,
the judge of all, and to the spirits of righteous men made
perfect, and to the sprinkled blood, which speaks better
than the blood of Abel."*

One is hard pressed to make the Zionist announcement to
move their capital to Jerusalem, "an astounding fulfillment of
prophecy."

THE BLESSING

The third element of the promise to Abraham is that God
would bless Abraham as well as make him a blessing. We
have a promise of blessing TO and of a blessing coming
THROUGH this man and his seed. It is the latter that stands in
the climactic position in the paragraph of Genesis 12:1-3. God
said He would mediate a blessing to the rest of the world
through Abraham, "In you all the families of the earth shall be
blessed." This promise is repeated and reaffirmed and related
to the seed and clarified in Gen. 18:17,18 and Gen. 22:15,16;
26:2-4; 28:13,14.

Although it is not my intention to discuss at length the
Messianic Prophecies and their fulfillment, it is essential we
understand the Biblical statements and interpretations of the
Abrahamic covenant and promises as viewed by the writers
of the Old and New Testaments. So we note that this third
element, the promise to bless all nations through Abraham, is
said to be fulfilled in Jesus Christ. Acts 3:25,26:

*"And you are the heirs of the prophets and of the
covenant God made with your fathers. He said to Abraham, 'Through your offspring all peoples on earth will be
blessed.' When God raised up HIS servant, He sent Him
first to you to bless you by turning each of you from your
wicked ways."*

The Paulinian letter to the church at Galatia also corroborates that Christ is the fulfillment of the blessing portion of the promise made to Abraham and Israel. In Galatians 3:8:

> *"And the Scripture, forseeing that God would justify the Gentiles by faith, preached the Gospel beforehand to Abraham, saying, 'All the nations shall be blessed in you.'"*

It is evident that the important focal point of the Covenantal Promise made by God to Abraham was never the land, or the physical nation of Israel, but the potentiality of worldwide redemption and reconciliation through the advent of the Messiah. The inheritance spoken of is a spiritual one, not a material utopia. The "sons of Abraham," heirs according to promise, are those men and women of faith in the Messiah, regardless of race or ethnic origin. Again the air is cleared by the Galatian writer in Galatians 3:13,14:

> *"Christ redeemed us from the curse of the Law, having become a curse for us—for it is written, "Cursed is everyone who hangs on a tree"—in order that in Christ Jesus the blessing of Abraham might come to the Gentiles, so that we might receive the promise of the Spirit through faith."*

For some 3500 years the Jews considered all who were not descendants of Abraham to be Gentiles. It is these Gentiles who are the recipients of the promises made to Abraham, that is, those who accept Christ as God's Divine Son and the World's Messiah. All men are combined within the concept of faith in Christ and all distinctions or exceptions are assimilated. Again, Galatians 3:28:

> *"There is neither Jew nor Greek, there is neither slave nor free man, there is neither male nor female; for you are all one in Christ Jesus."*

The promise of Canaan was but a small and transitory part of the total plan of God, as is true of the entire history of Israel as a nation. Israel was not called to be an end in itself, but a means to an end; to be a servant of God through whom the world could receive the Sacred Scriptures as the Word of God, and Jesus Christ according to the flesh as the Saviour of the world.

WHO WERE THE DESCENDANTS OF ISRAEL

It seems generally agreed among popular interpreters that the covenantal promises were restricted and reserved for the Jews alone. But other possibilities do exist which merit our consideration. As we return to the biblical account of Abraham and his children, we find that the very first child born to Abraham was of Hagar, an Egyptian servant of his wife Sarah. The son born of Hagar was named by an attending angel in Genesis 16:10,11:

> *"Moreover, the angel of the Lord said to her, 'I will greatly multiply your descendants so that they shall be too many to count.' The angel of the Lord said to her further, 'Behold, you are with child, And you shall bear a son; And you shall call his name Ishmael, Because the Lord has given heed to your affliction."*

The son is named Ishmael, meaning "God hears." Now examine closely the angelic statement, "I will greatly multiply your descendants so that they shall be too many to count." This promise comes some thirteen years prior to the birth of Isaac. The Hebrew absolute infinitive functions here: "multiplying I will multiply" = "I will greatly multiply."

Archaeological discoveries have fully substantiated the details of this incident which occurred some eighteen or twenty centuries prior to the beginning of the Christian era. The practice of a slave woman bearing a child for a childless wife may seem strange to one in the Western world, but it was a common practice in the patriarchal world. Two primary sources confirm the practice, those being the Code of Hammurabi and the Nuzi tablets. From Paragraph 146 of the Hammurabi Code we learn that a priestess of certain rank who was free to marry but not to bear children, gave her husband a slave girl in order to provide him with a son.

Published texts of the Nuzi Tablets tell of a socially prominent family in which the wife who is childless is required to provide a slave girl as concubine in order that the husband may have an heir.

The wife, however, will have legal rights to the offspring. Moreover, if the formerly childless couple should later have a child of their own, they could not thrust out the child of the secondary wife. This is an exact parallel of the Genesis narrative. So we find a direct prophecy from God, administered by an angel, which promised vast multiplication of an Egyptian woman's son, whose father was Abraham. Here we have the birth of the Arab nation in full agreement with the will of God. From the very beginning, the Arabs (Ishmaelites) were to be free, intractable and PERMANENT! Ishmael and his descendants were to maintain an independent standing before all (in the presence of) the descendants of Abraham. History has confirmed this promise.

In the next chapter (Genesis 17), God reveals the promise and the covenant to Abraham. God promised to make many nations from Abrahams sons, *both* Ishmael and Isaac. The following text clearly indicates that Ishmael is not to be "disinherited" or overlooked in God's blessing and promise. Genesis 17:20

"As for Ishmael, I have heard you; behold, I will bless him, and will make him fruitful, and will multiply him exceedingly. He shall become the father of twelve princes, and I will make of him a great nation."

Ishmael was the reputed father of a large number of Arab tribes. Ishmael had twelve sons, who gave rise to as many tribes or nations called by their names, and who dwelt southward in Arabia. Moses names the twelve sons of Ishmael in Genesis 25:12-18. The noted historian Eusebius in 350 A.D. speaks of twelve Arabian Princes in his lifetime. The Arab descendents of Ishmael were indeed multiplied as God had promised with the emergence of the Nabateans, Itureans, Saracens, Ishmaelites, etc. All of the Arab peoples were strong in character and noble warriors. The Saracens possessed the civilized world for more than 300 years. Every noted conqueror, whether Hebrew, Egyptian, Assyrian, Chaldean, Persian, Grecian, Roman, Tartar, or Turkish, has pushed his conquest to their borders, but not one has ever been able to subdue them, or deprive them of their freedom. The mighty Shishak, King of Egypt whom we mentioned in Chapter 1, was obliged to draw a line along their frontiers for the protection of his kingdom from their raids. The descendants of Ishmael were divided into tribes, after the manner of the Jews, differing however in disposition, habit and character. An Arab's word has always been his bond, and it remains so today. Many of the Arab tribes made great advances in early civilization and learning, and exhibited the ordinary aspect of powerful, settled, and regular communities. A vast number of these early Arab settlers, of whom the Bedouins are most generally known, who have, in all ages, practically and literally realized the prediction of the angel and God occurring later in chapter seventeen. They lived, and still do, in a state of uninterrupted freedom, seeking no home but the desert, submitted to no law but the Koran and their own will.

We will soon see that the prophecies concerning the Jews and Arabs are not at all what we hear being taught as truth today. As we read Deuteronomy 28:64, "the Lord will scatter you among all peoples, from one end of the earth to the other," we learn that the child of the promise, the descendants of Isaac will NOT REMAIN IN THE LAND! But rather, it is Ishmael and his descendants who WILL REMAIN IN THE LAND (Gen. 16:12). While Israel is scattered, dispersed and outcast, Ishmael will abide in the land promised to Hagar. Israel is scattered in judgment as chaff of the thrashing-floor; Ishmael abides immovable as Sinai. (See Luke 21:24, Acts 17:6.)

Though it is true that the specific covenant and spiritual promise was exclusively stated to be between Isaac and his offspring in Genesis 17:21, the promise to bless Ishmael still remains intact. It is the promise of the Messiah through Isaac's descendants that is special. After receiving God's desire for those who would be a part of this covenant be circumcised, Abraham immediately carries out this command. Genesis 17:23:

"On that very day Abraham took his son Ishmael and all those born in his household, and circumcised them, as God told him."

Thus it was Ishmael who was circumcised at thirteen years of age, before Isaac was born. (Gen. 17:25) Now if Ismael, the first-born was circumcised by Abraham as a part of the covenant with God, how can anyone believe that he (Ishmael) and his Arab descendants were somehow, somewhere, disinherited from the promises already given to Hagar and Ishmael? It is sometime later during the time of Isaac and Jacob that the promise is narrowed to their descendants, though again not in such a way as to totally exclude their Arab brethren; and it is a well known fact that many Arabs accompanied Moses and Joshua into Palestine when the country was partially occupied; and much of Moses' success was due at least in part to the kindness and hospitality of Jethro the Midianite who was, of course, an Arab and Moses' father-in-law. (Exodus 3:1)

HISTORICAL FULFILLMENT OF THE LAND PROMISE

When interpreting prophecy, we must see that prophecy first in its own historical setting and situation. Interpretation begins with the historically contemporaneous aspect of the prophecy. It may be that the prophecy does not project beyond the immediate historical situation. It may well have already found an adequate fulfillment in the past historical occurrences.

Was the land promise fulfilled in the events of past history? ABSOLUTELY! God repeated the promise of the land inheritance on numerous occasions, as originally found in Genesis 12:7:

"To your offspring I will give this land."

There is no indication whatosever of a two-fold land promise, or a division of the promise which would mean one land promise fulfilled in the lifetime of Abraham and Isaac, and a second "land promise" or sometimes called "Larger Land of Canaan" which is now being fulfilled by the present-day Jewish occupation of Palestine. Those who believe this double promise insist God kept only PART of the promise to Abraham by leading the children of Israel on their Exodus from Egypt in 1440 B.C. into Palestine. The Zionist military government is busy fulfilling the "larger land" promise, part two. *THIS IS ABSOLUTELY FALSE!* As I have stated, the biblical text contains in no location a "dual promise." The one and only promise repeated by God was the occupation of ancient Canaan. A basic rule of hermeneutics applies to this inference; no distinctions can be made where there is no difference in the text!

When Abraham arrived in what was called Canaan, it was already occupied by its earliest inhabitants, the Canaanites. The country was named after these inhabitants who were direct descendants of Canaan the son of Ham. Recall our earlier discussions of the original inhabitants of Palestine among whom were the Canaanites, a people of Semitic stock and were part of the large migration of Semitic tribes from Arabia.

When Abraham arrived in Canaan, the Lord appeared to him and reaffirmed the promsie of Gen. 12:7. In Genesis 13:14,15 we read:

> *"Lift up your eyes from where you are and look North and South, East and West. All the Land you see I will give to you and your offspring forever."*

This description of the boundaries of the 'promised land' is what is called by some, the "larger land of Canaan." But you will notice it was referred to as the covenant given to Abraham.

DID GOD INTEND ABRAHAM, ISAAC, AND JACOB TO INHERIT THE LAND PERSONALLY? If so, is it not strange that God made no attempt to give it to them. God keeps His promises, and most certainly would have given the land to them personally if He so intended. ABRAHAM HAD THE COVENANT, BUT NOT THE LAND. The land promise belonged within what some might call the 'Exodus situation', the beginnings of the Hebrew nation. Just as the promise of a numerous seed had been fulfilled in Egypt during the 500 years of slavery, so the promise of a land was fulfilled when

Israel conquered and possessed Canaan under the leadership of Joshua.

Prior to their (the Jews) entering the land, God said in Deut. 1:8:

> "See, I have placed the land before you; go in and possess the land which the Lord swore to give to your fathers, to Abraham, to Isaac, and to Jacob, to them and their descendants after them."

The land promise was fulfilled. Joshua refers to this fulfillment in his farewell message to his people in Joshua 23:14:

> "Now behold, today I am going the way of all the earth and you know in all your hearts and in all your souls that not one word of all the good words which the Lord your God spoke concerning you has failed; all have been fulfilled for you, not one of them has failed."

Joshua calls the land a good land, in their possession in Joshua 23:15:

> "this good land which He has given you."

There is no need for anyone today to look beyond that fulfillment as far as the original promise is concerned. GOD KEPT HIS PROMISE TO GIVE THE LAND. The promise in Genesis and Exodus, understood in its historical context, was, and has been, fulfilled. It is not "yet to be fulfilled." Israel literally possessed the Land. The final, declarative statement is found in Joshus 21:43:

> "So the Lord gave Israel all the land which He had sworn to give to their fathers, and they possessed it and lived in it."

Not only was the land portion of the promise fulfilled, but according to Joshua, the entire physical covenant, as in Joshua 21:45:

> "Not one of the good promises which the Lord had made to the house of Israel failed; all came to pass."

THE COVENANT CONDITIONS

The land covenant which God made with Abraham and subsequently to all Israel was, like all covenants made between two parties, conditional, and would be fulfilled ONLY IF BOTH PARTIES KEPT THE CONDITIONS SPECIFIED IN THE COVENANT! God always kept His commitments, but Israel historically, failed to meet the conditions which God placed on the covenant.

In respect to the land covenant, God promised a land-home for Israel, to be retained AS LONG AS ISRAEL OBEYED THE LAW OF MOSES. Conversely, God also *promised* they (Israel) would forfeit the covenant, which included the land promise, if they disobeyed Him and did not keep His Law as delivered through Moses. The land was to be Israel's as long as they remained spiritual Israel, and until they would fulfill their role as predecessors for the coming Messiah.

God does not order human history about in such a way that each man or nation is a mere puppet mechanically manipulated on the stage of life or world history. God sets the conditions and issues the guidelines for the task; He reveals the goal or promised reward; but He also reveals the punishment, the negative deeds or activities one can expect if those same rules and guidelines are in anyway impeached or abrogated.

The covenant stipulated and embraced no more than did the promise under which it was made. It was a ratification, or acceptance on their part, of the stipulations of the promise. It was the covenant by which God renewed His promise to be their God, and by it the people accepted the offer, and covenanted to be the people of God. This covenant bound both parties to their pledge; God to be their God; Israel to be His obedient people. It did not, and could not stipulate and grant more than did the promise; thus, all these were temporal in their nature.

This completed all that God had to provide for that people. From that point forward, there was nothing for either party to do, but to carry out the provisions of the covenant. But the people broke their part of the covenant, and a covenant broken on one side, is broken on both.

When God makes man a promise, He expects the response of the obedience of faith if the individual concerned is to possess the blessing. To determine how serious Abraham took the covenantal promise to him and his descendants, God gave him one final test recorded in Genesis 22:15-18. God asked Abraham to offer his long-awaited son as a burnt offering. When Abraham was prepared to carry out God's command, God told him he and his descendants will inherit the promises because Abraham was ready to obey God's command for the sacrifice of his son. God says "because you have obeyed my voice." The conditional covenant is reiterated in Exodus 19:5,6:

> *"Now then, if you will indeed obey My voice and keep My covenant, then you shall be My own possession among all the peoples, for all the earth is Mine; and you shall be to Me a kingdom of priests and a holy nation. These are the words that you shall speak to the sons of Israel."*

God would not make use of Israel as a "kingdom of priests" if they persisted in disobedience; nor would they experience His blessings without faith. To illustrate the common and frequent connection of promise and obedience given simultaneously, consider the entire chapter twenty-eight of Deuteronomy. In Deut 28:1:

> *"If you fully obey the Lord your God and carefully follow all His commandments I give you today, the Lord your God will set you high above all the nations of the earth."*

The specific promises are then given after Deuteronomy 28:2:

> *"And all these blessings shall come upon you and overtake you if you will obey the Lord your God."*

Notice that preparatory to listing the numerous blessings God is prepared to give the people, the emphasis of the opening remarks of this important chapter stress the condition of obedience and faithfulness, rather than the rewards. For the next twelve verses of this chapter, Moses records the tremendous blessings to be theirs as a result of faithful obedience. But when we arrive at verse fifteen, we encounter the promise of destruction:

> *"But it shall come about, if you will not obey the Lord your God, to observe to do all His commandments and His statutes which I charge you today, then all these curses shall come upon you and overtake you."*

I encourage you to read the entire twenty-eighth Chapter of Deuteronomy. Fourteen verses reiterate the Promises of God, BUT THE REMAINING FIFTY-FOUR VERSES EMPHASIZE THE DRASTIC CURSES AND TRAGIC EFFECTS WHICH WERE TO ACCOMPANY THE JEWS IF THEY DID NOT KEEP THEIR PART OF THE BARGAIN. One must ask, did the Jews keep the Law and ordinances of God? The answer is recorded for all posterity in the same historical record which speaks of the glowing promises and rewards to be received by obedient people. The Bible clearly reveals the falling away, the worshipping of false Gods, the absolute perversion of the nation of Israel in totality. The names of the individuals and tribes are there; the cities and locations of their depravities are there; yet it seems that many who support the prophecy proposition of Israeli occupation of Palestine have somehow failed to read it! Time after time the Jews abrogated their part of the agreed covenant.

If God keeps His word and promises, then we must inquire of the biblical record and secular history to determine if His promises of death and destruction were carried out against the Jews for their failure to follow through in their covenantal obligations. If you will recall our discussion of the dispersion of the Jews which is a fact of recorded history, we learned that not only did the Jews break their part of the covenant, but the calamities *PROMISED BY GOD* did indeed occur. God does keep His promises, both positive and negative!

> *"Moreover, the Lord will scatter you among all peoples, from one end of the earth to the other end of the earth; and there you shall serve other gods, wood and stone, which you or your fathers have not known. And among those nations you shall find no rest, and there shall be no resting place for the sole of your foot; but there the Lord will give you a trembling heart, failing of eyes, and despair of soul. So your life shall hang in doubt before you; and you shall be in dread night and day, and shall have no assurance of your life." Deuteronomy 28:64-66*

This amazingly accurate description of the captivities and the Diaspora of the Jews, even until this very day, settle once and for all the question as to the Jews inhabiting the land and then losing it through their own disobedience. Deuteronomy 28:21:

> *"The Lord will make the pestilence cling to you until He has consumed you from the land, where you are entering to possess it."*

After 500 years of possession of the land, Israel was once again dispossessed. The Jews went into exile, the Northern Kingdom going into the Assyrian Captivity in 722 B.C., and the Southern Kingdom going into the Babylonian Captivity in 586 B.C. We discussed these captivities in Chapter 1, and noted they were predicted by the Prophets. But the prophets predicted a return from captivity as well. It is this predicted return that many today assert to be in active fulfillment by the emerging of the Jewish state of Israel. But this concept is not contained in the biblical text and is, in fact, in opposition to the historical facts.

DID THE JEWS RETURN?
IS THEIR RETURN STILL TO COME?

The promise was explicit, and was explicitly fulfilled when the Jews did return from the Babylonian exile and rebuilt the city of Jerusalem and the great Temple.

> *"For the Lord says, 'When seventy years have been completed for Babylon, I will visit you and fulfill My good word to you, to bring you back to this place. For I know the plans that I have for you,' declares the Lord, 'plans for welfare and not for calamity to give you a future and a hope. Then you will call upon Me and come and pray to Me, and I will listen to you. And you will seek Me and find Me, when you search for Me with all your heart. And I will be found by you,' declares the Lord, 'And I will restore your fortunes and will gather you from all the nations and from all the places I have driven you,' declares the Lord, 'and I will bring you back to the place from where I sent you into exile." Jeremiah 29:10-14*

A close parallel passage is found in Isaiah 52:7-12. Nearly all the prophets write in anticipation of or actually partook in the Babylonian captivity. They shall return. God will perform a new Exodus. They shall possess the land again. Jeremiah 30:18, 31:17:

"Thus says the Lord, 'Behold I will restore the fortunes of the tents of Jacob and have compassion on his dwelling places; and the city shall be rebuilt on its ruin, and the palace shall stand on its rightful place.

"And there is hope for your future," declares the Lord, "And your children shall return to their own territory."

In the year 457 B.C. an executive order was issued by King Artaxerxes instructing the Jews to return, rebuild and reoccupy the land of Palestine. An exact copy of this decree to restore and rebuild Jerusalem has been discovered. The cylinder of Cyrus also records the forthcoming return of the Jews from captivity, and rebuilding the temple. (See Bibliography and Suggested Reading lists.)

As one becomes familiar with the many archaeological findings and their precise corroboration of this return an inescapable conclusion is reached: THE LAND PROMISE HAS BEEN FULFILLED ENTIRELY! There is no "restoration of the land" still due the Jews of today. Nor were the Jews to possess the land the second time "forever," anymore than their first possession. Like the first occupation and covenant, it was conditional upon their continued faithfulness to and observation of God's Law. History records their final demise once again, and their total dissemination by the Roman Army beginning in 63 B.C. when Pompey conquered Palestine for the Roman Empire.

Every "proof-text" submitted by Jews today or misguided, naive Christians in support of the occupation of Palestine is an attempt to prove that Christ will establish a Jewish Kingdom in Palestine, therefore the Jews have a biblical right to the land. Surely we have found this to be an extremely poor exegesis as well as highly misleading to many. The Kingdom is, as Jesus said, "not of this world." And the "earthly kingdom" scenario completely fails to correctly receive the intended meanings of the Messianic prophecies, even as the

Jews of Christ's day rejected Him as the Messiah simply because He did not "fit" their ideas and "interpretations" of how the Messiah of Israel (and the world) would act and live.

If there is any unfulfilled element in the prophecies relative to the Jews, it is not in relationship to externals, but the failure to achieve the spiritual reality that was the original goal of the covenant. God kept His word and His promise to give them the land on His conditions. It is done, and it is finished.

There remains not one single unfulfilled promise or prophecy as to the Jews being promised a home in Palestine. Every "proof-text" was either not fulfilled because Israel defaulted the covenant by disobedience, or the promise or prophecy has been fulfilled either in the first occupation of Canaan or the second occupation following the Babylonian captivity.

"BUT IT WAS PROMISED TO THEM FOREVER"

Those who purport the term "forever" somehow proves the land is still to belong to the Jews of today, irregardless of the fact that none of them can claim to be of the original Hebrews of the Exodus, these same "literalists" must likewise accept the "forever" requirement associated with the covenant, that of the rite of circumcision. This, too, was said to be "forever" in Genesis 17:10,14:

"This is My covenant, which you shall keep, between Me and you and your descendants after you: every male among you shall be circumcised."

"But an uncircumcised male who is not circumcised in the flesh of his foreskin, that person shall be cut off from his people; he has broken My covenant."

But do those claimants supporting a Jewish state advocate that the accompanying rite of circumcision must also be carried out on every Jewish male? Is there anyone today who would dare insinuate that all are still to be circumcised, and that circumcision is an eternally valid and necessary ordinance and a sign of a covenantal relationship with God? Even the Old Testament writers knew better! Moses in Deuteronomy and the prophet Jeremiah spoke of circumcision OF THE HEART, implying a purely spiritual experience is more significant than the external circumcision of the flesh.

IIn Deuteronomy 10:16: "Circumcise your heart, and stiffen your necks no more." The New Testament writers likewise understood that the seal of the covenant was not fleshly, but of a spiritual nature. Paul the Apostle is quite explicit in Romans 2:28,29:

> *"A man is not a Jew if he is one outwardly; neither is circumcision that which is outward in the flesh. But he is a Jew who is one inwardly; and circumcision is that which is of the heart, by the Spirit, not by the letter; and his praise is not from men, but from God."*

Paul goes a bit further by stating in Galatians 5:6:

> *"For in Christ Jesus neither circumcision nor uncircumcision means anything, but faith working through love."*

Biblical scholars would do well to spend an afternoon with an analytical concordance researching the biblical usage of the Hebrew word 'olam' and its Greek counterpart 'aion'. Although 'berith olam' is used to mean "everlasting covenant," and 'achuzath olam' to mean "everlasting land," most of them (scholars) would be aghast to learn that while olam is translated by such words as "ever lasting" and "ever more," it really does not refer to endless duration. Rather, it simply means "age-lasting." The Greek counterpart 'aion' normally means an "age." Take for example, Deuteronomy 15:17:

> *"Then you shall take an awl and pierce it through his ear into the door, and he shall be your servant FOREVER."* ('olam')

Obviously the meaning is for as long as the servant lives, which is subject to limitation. A number of the ages referred to were not, obviously, long lasting. Joshua 8:28:

> *"Joshua burned Ai and made it a heap forever, a desolation until this day."*

We know Ai was reinhabited and rebuilt after the time of Joshua for men of Ai returned from Babylon with Zerubbabel (Ezra 2:28).

Likewise, the Sabbath law which served as the centralizing focal point for the Mosaic system including the required rituals, sacrifices and feasts, was given "forever." It was to be observed "in all your generations" even "perpetually." Yet very few (if any) of the major Jewish state supporters practice Saturday worship or animal sacrifices. Why not? The same term (olam) is used for them? Would the "land grant literalists" really want to argue that even beyond the endless ages of the world, even beyond the cosmic order of the universe, that Israel is supposed to dwell in the land promised to Abraham? There are numerous "olam ordinances," but these advocates are quite selective about which ones they choose to obey and which they will reject. I know of NONE who offer animal sacrifice for their sin.

Yet there is no reason to assume the 'olam' used in association with the land promise is any different from its other uses elsewhere in the Bible.

THE SPIRITUAL BLESSING AND
TWO COVENANTS CONSIDERED

How was Abraham to become a multitude of nations? Such was the central part of the promise of God in Genesis 17:1-17. Even if we consider the whole of the twelve sons of Jacob and their history, we find they founded ONLY THE ONE NATION of Israel, with which Jehovah established the covenant made with Abraham, so that Abraham became through Israel the lineal father of ONE NATION ONLY. Does it not follow that the posterity of Abraham, which was to expand into a multitude of nations, must extend beyond this one lineal posterity, and embraces the spiritual posterity also in that all nations are grafted (ex pisteos Abraam) into the seed of Abraham? By this enlargement it follows that in reality Abraham received the promise made by God, and stated in Romans 4:13:

"For the promise to Abraham and to his descendants that he would be heir of the world was not through the Law, but through the righteousness of faith."

"The promise that God would bless the whole world through Abraham had reference to Christ, the son of Abraham, through whom God would fulfill His promise of blessing the whole world through the offspring of Abraham. This promise was the first one made, but the last in fulfillment, with an interval of nearly 2000 years. It was ratified and covenanted by the blood of Christ, and looked to the possession of the heavenly Canaan, to a circumcision that cut off the heart from all that is worldly and sensual, and to a seal that became the pledge of the purchased possession, and its settlment in the heavenly Canaan, by the Resurrection from the dead, when the spiritual people of God cross the Jordan of death, and take possession of the land of promise, for which even Abraham looked, when he sought "a city whose maker and builder is God." (H. Christopher, The Remedial System, pg. 146)

It seems strange to believe that a land Israel lost because of their disobedience is to be regained while still unbelieving and disobedient. If anyone really believes the present-day Israelis are keeping the covenant of God made with Moses, they should take a tour of the "Holy Land" to quickly realize the error of their thinking. Not even the core of the covenant, the decalogue, is kept as commanded. Even the noted pro-Zionist/restorationist Walvoord, in his book "Israel in Prophecy" page 24 admits:

> *"It soon becomes evident to visitors that the religion of Israel is to some extent one of outward form. The religious exercises are devoted primarily to revival of their traditions, and the application to some extent of moral standards. For Israel their religion is one of works rather than of faith, and their redemption is to be achieved by their own efforts."*

The question seems to be, is the Old Law and Covenant still applicable and binding today? If the answer is no, then the Zionist occupation of Palestine is wrong and not supported by the Bible, let alone by God. If one answers in the affirmative, then ALL OF THE LAW AND COVENANTS MUST BE ADMINISTERED TODAY! There simply is no scripture giving anyone the convenient "perogative" to "pick and choose" among the laws and ordinances which accompany the Abrahamic Covenant and Land Promise.

We mentioned circumcision, but what about animal sacrifices, keeping the Passover, hallowing the seventh day, letting the lands "rest" every seventh year, sorting out "clean" and "unclean" animals, and establishing an order of the Levitical Priesthood. Capital punishment was usually inflicted for an infraction or disavowance of any of these statutes "given forever" by God to Abraham, Moses, and the children of Israel. Paul the Apostle refers to the Old Covenant as "the administration of death" in 2 Corinthians 3:7.

Again I must issue the challenge; there is not one single Christian church or organization which so proudly espouses Jewish Occupation of Palestine, yet keeps all of the remaining ordinances. Is this not an example of hyprocisy? Or perhaps it is really a direct result of poor biblical knowledge and blind, non-thinking acceptance of someone's favorite dogma and end-times scenario. These advocates are wise not to practice these statutes, for they are in no sense a part of the Christian Gospel or system anymore than the "land grant" to Abraham. All were intended for the FLESHLY seed of Abraham only, and were abrogated along with the Mosaic Law at the death of Christ.

For a thorough and hermeneutical study of the Old and New Covenants contained in the Old and New Testaments, I heartily recommend the book, "Genesis" Volume III, by Dr. C. C. Crawford. (See Bibliography.)

The prophecies of a return by a remnant of the dispersed Jews do not place prominence on regaining the land. There is a deepening spiritual note, making it clear that the essential part of the experience is a return to God; a renewal of their former covenantal relationship of blessing through forgiveness to a people now ready to respond to God's 'hesed' (Hebrew for steadfast love) with the obedience of faith. This "reunion" is expressed with poetical grandeur by Hosea in Hosea 2:14-20, where Israel is portrayed as the Bride of God in a joyous wedding.

Now, we are going to briefly examine the primary "proof-texts" used today and believed by far too many well meaning Christians, to "prove" and "validate" the Zionist Military

Governments continued aggression and occupation in Arab Palestine. Since we have already quoted many of the texts, I will simply list them first as they are written by their authors, and then cite the fulfillment of the prophecy either by historical verification or biblical fulfillment, with the correct biblical text which accomplished that fulfillment. I do urge the reader to satisfy his own mind and comprehension of the fulfilled prophecies which follow by looking up each one as listed. I also suggest one use either the New International Version or the New American Standard Bible for their study.The texts will be classified by the common Biblical periods of which they are a part.

I. MOSAIC PROPHIECIES (Approximately 900 years before Babylonian Captivity)

1. Deut. 4:27 was fulfilled in the captivity (Dt. 6:10-15)
2. Deut. chapters 28 through 30 was fulfilled in Israel's return from the Babylonian Captivity.
   (a) The promise was conditional. (Dt. 28:1,2)
   (b) Israel failed to keep the conditions, abrogating the Promise. (Dt. 28:62,63) Notice the terms, "Destroy you," "Bring you to nothing," "torn from the land."
   (c) God warned Israel she would not be spared (Dt. 28:29).
   (d) The parallel case of Solomon in I Chronicles 28:6-9. Because Solomon failed to meet the conditions, Israel was divided into two nations and eventually carried captive from the land home.
   (e) These passages found fulfillment in the Babylonian Captivity. Prophet Nehemiah cites this passage in Neh. 1:6-9. He claims its fulfillment in his time, and he was even then in captivity.
3. Leviticus 26:40-45 was fulfilled in Israel's return from captivity. This text refers to the Babylonian captivity. It has been fulfilled like all the others (Jer. 29:10-17).

II. PROPHECIES OF SAMUEL (400 years before the Babylonian Captivity)

1. II Samuel 7:12-16 is fulfilled, as stated in Hebrews 1:5.
2. I Chronicles 17:11 is fulfilled as revealed by Acts 2:29. Even though some claim it is still in the future, we must remember that an inspired statement that IT HAS BEEN FULFILLED is to be preferred above pre-millenial guesses.

III. PROPHECIES OF DAVID (400 years before the Babylonian Captivity)

1. Psalm 2 is fulfilled as evidenced by the following scriptures:
   (a) Verses 1,2 are quoted in Acts 4:24-26 in reference to Christ's first coming, crucifixion, and Kingship.
   (b) Verse 7 is quoted in Acts 13:33 in reference to Christ's Resurrection.
   (c) Verse 7 is also quoted in Hebrews 1:5 and 5:5 in reference to Christ's Priesthood.
2. Psalm 72, which is similar to Zechariah 9:9,10, is obviously fulfilled for the latter is quoted as fulfilled in Matthew 21:9.
3. Psalm 110 is fulfilled in Hebrews 5:6-10; 6:20; and 7:17.

IV. PROPHECIES OF ISAIAH (Over 100 years before Babylonian Captivity)

1. Isaiah 2 was fulfilled beginning on the Day of Pentacost. Isaiah 2:1-5 is fulfilled in Luke 24:46-49. Now Micah 4:1-7 is a prophecy identical with Isaiah 2:1-5 and either one or both were cited by Christ as referring to the Christian era and not a premillennial age!
2. Isaiah 11:1-10 is fulfilled as stated in Acts 13:22-24 and Romans 12:12. The Prophecy is Isaiah 11:1-10. This is identical to parts of Micah 4:1-7. Premillennialists insist on interpreting this literally. Now if the animals are to be taken literally, then the "Branch" of vs 10 and the "Holy Mountain" of vs 9 are also to be taken literally. If not, why not? And if not, what shall we take literally? Verse 9 does not teach universal peace, but universal knowledge. Reference is made

to the Church (Isa. 1-4; Heb. 12:22,23; Col. 1:23; Romans 10:18) and is fulfilled in the Gentiles seeking Christ.

FULFILLMENT
    (a) Verse 1 is cited in Acts 13:22-24 as having been fulfilled in the Christian era, not a premillennial time.
    (b) Verse 10 is cited in Romans 12:1,2 as having been fulfilled in the Christian era, not a premillennial theory.
3. Isaiah 18 is fulfilled as the context shows. Note the series of chapters in which this prophecy is set.
    (a) Chapter 13....the destruction of Babylon.
    (b) Chapter 14....the destruction of Philistia.
    (c) Chapter 15....the destruction of Moab.
    (d) Chapter 17....the destruction of Damascus.
    (e) Chapter 18....the destruction of Ethiopia.
    (f) Chapter 19....the destruction of Egypt.
All of these are either future or all are history. They were future when prophesied, but history now fulfilled.
4. Isaiah 28:14-16 is fulfilled in Romans 9:33, I Peter 2:6 and Ephesians 2:20.
5. Isaiah 31:1-5 evidences its own fulfillment as it is merely a warning against Israel making an alliance with Egypt.
6. Isaiah 55:3 is fulfilled in Acts 13:33,34.
7. Isaiah 65:17-20 is fulfilled as the many parallel passages clearly indicate.

V. PROPHECIES OF JEREMIAH...He prophesied during the Jerusalem Siege, prior to the Babyloanian Captivity. His prophecies were fulfilled in Israel's Return from Captivity.
1. Jeremiah 23:5-8 is fulfilled in Christ (see parallel passages).
    (a) Zechariah 6:13 is a comparative passage, and it has been fulfilled as a reference to earlier messages will show.
    (b) Isaiah 11:1 likewise a comparative passage, is

fulfilled as the same reference will show.
2. Jeremiah 25:11-13 is fulfilled by reading II Chronicles 30:20-23 and Ezra 1:1-4.

VI. EZEKIEL...Prophesied during Israel's Exile in Babylon.
The Prophecy...Ezekiel 36:16-28
The Fulfillment:
   (a) Ezekiel's prophecies referred to the Babylonian Captivity. (Ezekiel 3:11, 12:13, 19:9)
   (b) The Law was then in force, and was involved in Ezekiel's prophecies. (Ezekiel 36:25, 36:38)
   (c) Premillennialists commonly refer to Chapters 34, 36, and 37, but they were totally fulfilled in Israel's return from the Captivity.

VII. DANIEL...Prophesied during Israel's Exile in Babylon.
Prophecies...Daniel 2:44 and 7:13,14.
Fulfillment:
   (a) Mark 1:14 and Hebrews 12:28. Christ declared that these time-prophecies were filled to the full, and Paul affirmed that the Kingdom had arrived.

VI. MINOR PROPHETS...Numerous prophets prophesied prior to, during, and immediately following the Babylonian Captivity. Their prophecies are either fulfilled in the captivity or are given in figurative languge and refer to the Church and Heaven.
   (a) Joel 3:9-14 refers to the end of Israel's captivity.
       Prophecy...Joel 3:9-14
       Fulfillment...Joel 3:1,2. Clearly refers to captivity.
   (b) Amos 9:13-15 is fulfilled in Acts 15:13-17.
       Prophecy...Amos 9:13-15
       Fulfillment...Acts 15:13-17. Gentiles could not be saved if this text were not fulfilled.
   (c) Nahum 2:3,4 refers to ancient Nineveh.
       Prophecy...Nahum 2:3,4
       Fulfillment...Nahum 1:1...A similar reference was made to Tyre and Judah, and it is evident they are fulfilled.

(d) Zechariah 1:14-18 is fulfilled according to the text.
(e) Zephaniah 3:8 refers to the punishment to be visited upon Jerusalem following the last captivity.
Fulfillment...Zephaniah 3:20.
(f) Zechariah 8:10 refers to the rebuilding of the temple of Zerubbabel.
Prophecy...Haggai 2:13,14
Fulfillment...Comparative passages of Ezra 5:1, Ezra 6:14 and II Chronicles 15:3-6.

The literalistic or premillennialist theories do great harm to several fundamental and basic biblical truths as well as continuing to render irrational support for the Occupation of Palestine and the displacement of the Arab Palestinian People.

(1) This view would make the restored nation of Israel today to keep the Law of Moses, which was "made full" and/or abrogated by Jesus Christ and the New Covenant. Deuteronomy 30:1-10 will reveal to the reader that the only promise of a restoration of the nation included adherence and obedience to the Law of Moses. Not only the promise, but the only actual and historically documented restoration likewise indicates the returned Jews were under the Law of Moses.

Also, the promise in Deuteronomy, chapters 28-30 demanded Israel FIRST be converted before they will return. The literalists say they will first RETURN and THEN be converted. The fact is, not even the wildest and most fanciful of the popular literalist writers can say, with a straight face, that "all the Jews are returning to Israel." (See Chapter 3.)

(2) Literalists ignore the plain teaching that the NATION OF BIBLICAL ISRAEL WILL NOT BE RESTORED! They tend to conveniently overlook the following passages which teach that the biblical nation of Israel would be so utterly dissolved that it would never again be intact nor inhabit the land of promise.

(a) Hosea 1:4-6
(b) Isaiah 5:1-6
(c) Jeremiah 19:1-11; 23:39,40

(d) Matthew 21:33-45
(e) Matthew 23:37,38

Christ Himself taught He would grind to powder those of whom He spoke, and the Jews "understood that He was speaking about them" in Matthew 21:45.

(3) The Premillennial/Literal theory overlooks the IMPOSSIBILITY of reallotment of the land to a nation. Land inheritance was given and retained solely through family estates, which have been totally lost long ago. (Joshua 24:28; Leviticus 25:23-28) Herod the Great destroyed all Jewish geneologies and God further forbids them in the Gospel Dispensation. I Timothy 1:4:

"nor pay attention to myths and endless GENEOLOGIES, which give rise to mere speculation rather than further-ing the administration of God which is by faith"

(4) This distorted interpretation makes a distinction where none really exists. The Bible clearly, completely teaches there is no difference between Jews and Gentiles today. Consider the following texts which absolutely confirm this point:
(a) Acts 10:34; 15:9
(b) Romans 2:28,29; 10:12,13
(c) I Corinthians 12:13
(d) Galatians 3:26-28
(e) Ephesians 2:11-19

God will not save one nation by the proclamation of the Gospel and another nation through personal persuasion. This stands in arrogant opposition to the entire teaching of the New Testament regarding the New Covenant and God's Plan of Redemption for All Mankind!

(5) Premillennial/Literal theories corrupt the True Israel of God. New Testament Israel is not the old fleshly Israel, but is now Spiritual Israel, the Church. It is "Spiritual Israel" which is now the recipient of the Covenant of God. Two important texts illustrate this fact:

"For neither is circumcision anything, nor uncircum-cision, but a new creation. And those who will walk by this rule, peace and mercy be upon them, and upon the Israel of God." (Galatians 6:15,16)

"But you are a chosen race, a royal priesthood, a holy nation, a people for God's own possession, that you may proclaim the excellencies of Him who has called you out of the darkness into His marvelous light; for you once were not a people, but now you are the people of God; you had not received mercy but now you have received mercy." (I Peter 2:9,10)

Old Testament Israel, as a NATION and as having any standing with God, has been destroyed. The only hope of Israel is salvation in heaven, not a home in Jerusalem. Acts 26:6,7; 28:20. The ancients have a far better place or abode than this physical earth to look forward to as evidenced in Hebrews 10:34; 11:16. Paul the Apostle counted the fleshly advantages of the Jews in him as "loss" for the sake of Jesus Christ. (Philippians 3:2-8)

(6) The Premillennial/Literal teaching confuses and contradicts the allegory given by Paul in Galatians 4:21-31. Please read this text, and you will see that the author clearly states that:

(a) The two women represent the two covenants...Old and New.
(b) The two sons represent the two nations... fleshly and spiritual.
(c) Verse 30: "Cast out the bondwoman (Old Covenant), and her son (fleshly Israel)."

There have always been two Israels in biblical prophecy, one fleshly and the other spiritual. Because the identity of the two Israels, and a recognition of their respective natures have not been consistently maintained and carefully considered in Biblical interpretation, exegetical error has prevailed with respect to prophecy's true application and manner of fulfillment. Not a few times have the "literalists" or the "premillennialists" endeavored to apply to fleshly Israel, in a material sense, what was intended for spiritual Israel in a nonmaterial sense. This accounts for the postponement theories that bypass the plain time statements of prophecy, and that anticipate a future national restoration of a fleshly Israel that will provide a literal or material fulfillment of such prophecies.

CONCLUSION

We began this chapter with a brief introduction to the science of Heremeneutics and discussion of some of the primary rules which must be known and employed in deriving the intended meaning of any biblical passage by any biblical author. By applying these principles, we have examined the major "proof texts" so often cited to support the present-day Zionist Government control over Palestine and its Arab inhabitants. These texts, when taken as written and intended by their authors, in no way substantiate the teachings and theories of those I have chosen to label "Literalists" and "Premillennialists," even though these teachings are quite popular among many fundamental Churches and their Pastors. What we have clearly learned is that there were indeed two covenants given by God, one a fleshly covenant and the other a spiritual covenant. The fleshly or physical Covenant (promise) was to fade away, but the Spiritual was to transcend and succeed the Old forever through the arrival of the promised and prophesied Messiah, Jesus Christ.

The original fleshly covenant made to the Jews and Abraham was not only temporary as respects the rights, privileges, and blessings which it secured to that people in that time; but it was also temporary in its duration. The people (Israel) broke that covenant. But it was faulty in that it only contemplated and provided for man's temporal needs and wants. Indeed, this was the fault of the whole Jewish fabric, from the inception to the close. This was foreseen, thus the whole structure was but a means to an end; a measure to give time for the preparation and institution of a better covenant. The promise of God under which the whole Jewish structure arose was not the first or chief promise that God made to Abraham, nor His chief purpose in calling him. The true and central promise to Abraham was that through him he would bless the whole human family. This promise was interpreted by the New Testament writers as having reference to Christ, and consequently, this new promise was to take precedence above the other promises.

The promise which pointed to Christ preceded the ratification of the land promise by several years, and antedated the

covenant of circumcision twenty-four years. The covenant at
Mt. Sinai followed the latter by some four hundred years. The
first and chief promise which contemplated spiritual blessings
and a spiritual offering through Isaac, was not ratified, or
covenanted, for nearly two thousand years! All that has
grown out of this promise has no connection with what arose
under the others. It differs from them in every respect. It has
differed from them in the very beginning. It came into the
world through a different line. There were two lines of
descendants in Isaac, as two promises were fulfilled in his
descendants. The one line was "the seed of Abraham according to the flesh," and the other "the seed according to the
spirit." The result of the two lines was Judaism and Christianity and both differ radically as to their nature, rights and
privileges, so much so as to exclude the one wholly from the
other.

The Creation, the Circumcision or seal, the purchase, and
the covenant that made Abraham and his descendants
according to the flesh the people of God, have no place nor
value under the Christian institution. The Christian institution
has its own creation and seal, its own purchase and covenant,
all of which are spiritual and eternal, and these give the
Christian no rights or privileges under the first or "older"
covenant.

As the spiritual and the eternal necessarily supersede the
fleshly and temporal, so does the Jewish institution, in whole
and in part, give way to the Christian. The Christian is a new
creation, and all that pertains to his creation is new. Before it
the Jews and Gentiles stand on the same ground. Both must
become the subjects of this new creation before they can be
regarded as belonging to the people of God. All the claims
which the Jew once preferred counts for nothing under the
operation of the new creation. A new birth is just as essential
for the Jew as for the Gentile. The Jewish birth of the flesh
avails nothing. Now, all that is acceptable to God is the new
creation in Christ His Son. The fleshly descendants or relatives, the family geneologies mean nothing in the new covenant and creation, for there is but one common denominator
for all men, Jesus Christ.

These things being true, all that is "Jewish" has passed away. The Jews are no longer the "people of God." Their whole religious service has perished along with their distinctive recognition as a nation among nations. What purpose God has now with that people remains to be seen. But it is clear that He has no further purpose with them in regard to the fulfillment of His promise of blessing the world through them by the Christ, the annointed Messiah, the Saviour of the World. Christianity has succeeded Judaism, and the whole religious service of Judaism perished with the total (and final) destruction of the temple in Jerusalem. Christ is the end of the Law, and of all that pertained to it. The law was but a pedagogue to lead the Jews to Christ, so that when He came, all that was Jewish was set aside, and the pedagogue was set aside or dismissed. All now become "the children of God" by faith in Christ Jesus, in whom "there is neither Jew nor Greek. There is neither slave nor free man, there is neither male nor female, for you are all ONE IN CHRIST JESUS!" (Galatians 3:28) And According to Paul the Apostle in Romans 4:13,16:

"For the promise to Abraham or to his descendants that he would be heir of the world was not through the law (flesh), but through the righteousness of faith."

"For this reason it is by faith, that it might be in accordance with grace, in order that the promise may be certain to all the descendants, not only to those who are of the Law, but also to those who are of the faith of Abraham, who is the father of us all."

It is done! The Old Promise, the Old Covenant made to Abraham and his descendants has been fulfilled COMPLETELY, IN TOTO! God has fully kept His word to Abraham and the original nation of Israel. They did indeed inherit and fully possess the "promised land" when the "children of Israel" entered Canaan under the direction of Moses and his successor, Joshua. The scriptures claim the fulfillment of all the physical and spiritual promises have occurred, and are complete. *GOD IS NOT RESTORING, FOR A SECOND TIME,* an assemblage of people who are only "Jewish" by choice or birth, and not on the basis of biblical or physical inheritance.

The biblical "nation," recipients of the physical land promises, were long ago scattered and assimilated among the nations of the world.

The teaching and emphasis of the Bible for today is the fulfillment and fruition of the Abrahamic promise by and through the appearance in time, space and history, of Jesus Christ. The Jew was the chosen of God only according to the flesh, and entitled only to the blessings of his covenant. The Jew is not the chosen of God according to the Spirit, or the seed of Isaac according to the promise.

I sincerely hope that every Bible reader and Christian believer will, upon concluding this chapter, re-examine and re-evaluate his acceptance of Premillennialist and Literalistic teaching which has so unjustly "forced" God to be in support of, indeed responsible for, the grievous injustice of the 'Theft of A Nation.'

Chapter 6

THE SEARCH FOR PEACE

"I, Menachem, the son of Zeer and Hasia Begin, do solemnly swear that as long as I serve the nation as Prime Minister, we will not leave any part of Judea, Samaria, the Gaza Strip, and the Golan Heights." May, 1981, West Bank of Palestine.

THUS WE HAVE the final edict as it were, of Mr. Begin and his Likud party which history will show, have done more to aggravate and exacerbate the Arab/Israeli conflict than perhaps any other government before them. The quote is taken from Newsweek Magazine, May 18, 1981. Perhaps this statement best represents the bellicosity and belligerance of the current government leaders who must be included in any talks or considerations which might lead to an ultimate settle-ment. How does one approach an adversary with the inten-tion of legitimate discussion and the pursual of peace when that adversary has crystalized his intransigence by publicizing his resistence to any deliberation which might require the return or restoration of the occupied land back to the original, lawful owners? What objectively are the prospects for arriv-ing at a just and equitable settlement when such an adamant attitude is expressed? I know of no European or Western Nation which would enter into serious dialogue with a long standing opponent knowing full well there is no hope for a reasonable agreement. The United States has demonstrated throughout its many wars and conflicts the necessity of "negotiation from a position of power" rather than weakness. Why should the Palestinians be expected to seek proper redress from a position of weakness? In fact, the strength or weakness of both middle east factions will determine whether they are prepared to accept the token offerings of their opponents, or to insist to the end that their just grievances must be addressed and alleviated.

The conflict continues as both the Jews and the Arabs battle for positions of strength in order to dictate any terms of peace. All the while the multiplied skirmishes and encounters contribute to a growing escalation of the conflict. Each side becomes even more entrenched in their refusal to negotiate with one another. There is no "good faith" on which to build a "good" settlement acceptable to all.

IS PEACE THROUGH DIPLOMACY EVEN POSSIBLE?

Diplomacy: "the art and practice of conducting negotiations between nations; (2) "skill in handling affairs without arousing hostility."

Here we have the definition as found in Webster's New Collegiate Dictionary, 1980 edition. Notice the section stating, "without arousing hostility." I submit that there can be no peace whatsoever until those elected representatives of the Israeli government cease and desist from their bold and purposeful insults and edicts against the Palestinian Arabs. Mr. Begin is especially well known to the world press for his insults and innuendos made publicly as if to purposely aggravate the delicate middle east balance of peace. Many European heads of government find it hard to see how the peace process can advance as long as Mr. Begin and his attitude continue. Why expect the Arab Palestinians to approach the peace table when they are informed time and again by childish bravado that Israel is unwilling to negotiate?

Before we can answer the question if peace is possible through diplomacy, we must first discuss what is meant by "peace." We all recognize that peace is not a concrete or visible structure which can be built brick by brick in accordance with an architect's blueprints. I believe peace is merely a symptom of the existence of healthy relations between human beings. This is true whether one speaks of peace among family members, neighbors, two neighboring nations or two separated nations. It is still the same, Peace among men or nations is brought about when normal, healthy relations exist. This same definition of peace applies to the Palestinian issue. And if ever there is to be a real and lasting peace between Arab and Jew, Zionist and Palestinian, it must be comprised of dialogue and exchange with one another.

For a true and just solution to be realized, both parties must enter into meaningful dialogue over substantive issues. It is quite irrelevant to permanent peace to speak of "secure boundaries" for boundaries are never secure; and it is likewise wrong and irrelevant to speak of one's "mighty and invincible army" for the annals of world history reveal the inability of any nation at any time to establish permanent peace without first establishing the prerequisite of healthy and respectful human relations. The only exception being when armies have annihilated one of the conflicting parties. Peace then becomes the peace of death, the peace of the graveyard.

The failure of force to produce peace in the Middle East is well illustrated in the swift, complete victory of Israel in June of 1967. As Jewish soldiers took over the West Bank cities, towns and villages, and eventually, the old city of Jerusalem, many thought that a lasting peace with the Arabs would immediately follow. But six years later, in 1973, the Egyptian Army crossed the Suez Canal and reclaimed much of the Sinai territory previously lost to Israel. As a result of the attempt to force a military peace, that sought after peace is now further away than ever before.

The Palestinians cannot forget the injustices received during the war and the subsequent occupation and are filled with bitterness and will attempt to remove the injustice by means of force. The fact that they have not yet achieved that goal is irrelevant, for it merely increases their desire to avenge their failures by an even greater effort against the Israelis. The Zionist government, having escaped persecution, and I believe being fully conscious of the injustices it has committed against the Palestinians, now fears retaliation and of course will resist any possible extermination in the new home they have established BY FORCE OF ARMS! As we have seen in the previous chapters of this book, Israel has sought self preservation and aggrandisement through the perpetuation and extension of the injustice by "appropriating" more land and establishing more settlements in Arab villages and towns. Under such conditions, how can "healthy human relations" exist between the two parties, let alone be promoted?

Before we can answer the original question as to whether peace is even possible through negotiation, we must answer a most critical and complex question: Can the injustice to the Palestinians be redressed without inflicting injustice on the Jewish nation and without threatening its continued existence? The answer to all of these questions is summed up in the term "JUSTICE." If true justice can be rendered to the Palestinians and their long-standing grievances, then reciprocal justice will be meted to the Israeli state from all aggrieved parties. Justice is the prerequisite for achieving the "human relations." Sadly, justice is sometimes defined, like right, in such a way as to support a specific point of view. When this occurs, justice becomes devoid of any ethical content and loses its effectiveness in producing the healthy human relations on which peace so greatly depends.

It would seem that a genuine search for peace must begin by answering two more fundamental questions: what are the dimensions of the injustice which has been inflicted on the Palestinians and second, what is a fair definition of justice in the context of the measures needed to properly redress this injustice? To the first question, I refer the readers to Chapters 2 and 3 where I listed the primary acts of injustice against the Palestianians. These included the cowardly "sell-out" by the British during World War I resulting in the Balfour Declaration, the Partition Mandate of the U.N. and subsequent theft of Palestinian lands, homes and businesses. You may wish, at this point, to return to those chapters for needed elucidation.

WHAT IS A FAIR DEFINITION OF
JUSTICE UNDER THE CIRCUMSTANCES?

As would be expected, both sides define real justice differently. The contemporary Palestinian assumes that everything done in Palestine after World War I by means of force or decree, against the will and wishes of the great majority of Palestinian Arabs then living in Palestine, were done illegally and were absolutely unjust. With this perspective and background, most Palestinians would define true justice and real conciliation along the following lines:

A. All Palestinians who were driven from their homes, lands and businesses in 1948 and again after the 1967 War should be permitted to return and once again possess those same lands and properties which were taken from them by force.

B. All Jews who entered Palestine during the British Mandate from 1917-1948 as well as those who entered after the establishment of Israel in 1948 should all return to the various countries of their origin.

C. Palestinians should be justly compensated for the use of their properties by the Jewish occupants who forced them to leave those same lands from 1948 until the present day.

D. That the Zionist state of Israel, established by force on the lands and in the homes of Palestinians should be dismantled and eventually eliminated.

E. That Jews should be allowed to retain only the original land they purchased legally, primarily during the British Mandate which would total some 1500 square kilometers (580 miles).

But the ordinary Israeli or Zionist certainly would not see this Arab proposal as true justice as far as their own future is concerned. As we have already discussed in Chapter 5, the Israelis have been telling the world and all who would listen, that the Jews have "a right" to Palestine guaranteed by the Bible. They also believe that all actions and proposals carried out by the United Nations including the use of force, are both legal and just. Their definition of true justice might be expressed in the following:

A. All lands, properties and businesses conquered by them in 1948 by force of arms legitimately belongs to them.

B. All territories captured by Israel in 1967 up to and including the present day, legitimately belongs to Israel and it is just for them to not only retain those lands, but to expropriate and retain any new lands or properties it may consider essential for its own security.

C. New seizures of Arab land is justifiable by reason of a need for new land to be available for newly arriving Jews who may come to Israel of their own volition or as a result of unfair persecution in their native country.

D. It is just that Jerusalem be placed under Israel's sovereignty and because it was once the capital of ancient Israel, it must once again be their capital. Most will admit that the holy and religious places should be accessible to all men and nations.

DIFFERENCES BETWEEN THE TWO DEFINITIONS

Study the previously stated definitions closely, and one will quickly recognize the one and only similarity between those items listed by Palestinians and Jews is their total diametric opposition. Is it possible for justice to be so imprecise that one person's definition is another's antithesis? If this be so, then one will search the world in vain without any hope of comprehending justice from injustice, right from wrong, truth from falsehood. Rather than accept such a negative premise, perhaps we can pursue the quest for justice from the given definitions by consideration of the basis from which both parties, Arab and Jew, have given them.

The Palestinians base their definition of justice on the interpretation given the term by the citizens of the world. Most dictionaries give a secondary rendering of justice as RIGHTEOUSNESS! And righteousness, whether used in a secular or biblical sense, denotes an attitude of absolute equity which leaves one without guilt. The international community has expressed such an attitude collectively over the many dark and sordid actions of men and nations carried out against innocent peoples. Whether one speaks of Adolf Hitler, Stalin, Chairman Mao or Idi Amin, all men recognized the trampling of justice beneath the feet of falsehood and deceit. It is from just such a position that the Palestinians have issued their justice definition. Their justice is the same justice found in the Fourteen Points enunciated by President Woodrow Wilson which helped bring an end to the first world war. The heart of these principles was respect and justice for men and nations. It is this respect and this justice which the Palestinians have sought.

Negatively, the Palestinians do not believe the victorious allies at the close of the war had any right or mandate to decide the direction or disposition of Palestine. They believe the actions of the old League of Nations and now the United Nations to be irrelevant. For no one, including foreign powers and persecuted religious bodies, had the right to initiate any actions against the will and wishes of the majority of Palestinian inhabitants. History clearly recounts how the politicized world governments ignored Wilson's fourteen points of justice and plunged a war-ravaged world population into a second and more terrifying disaster. This second world war sparked in several ways, the current conflict of the Middle East, as was discussed in Chapters 1 and 2.

The Jews base their definition on the claim of having an ancient and historic right to the land. Also, they claim the decisions of the League of Nations and the United Nations, namely the Balfour Declaration and the Partition Declaration, grant them the "legal" rights to the country, despite the fact that force was condoned to accomplish both acts. Certainly this "claim" is not based on any sense of justice.

The two points of view are so fundamentally opposed one must ask the question: can they ever be reconciled? Presidents, Kings, Prime Ministers and cabinets have attempted to bring about such a reconciliation for over sixty-five years to no avail. There will be no success until unbiased, neutrally objective outside statesmen propose a settlement which will institute human relationships acceptable between both parties.

CHOOSING SIDES. . .AN INTERNATIONAL PASTIME

When one refers to "sides" in the Middle East conflict, he must be certain to include all participants besides the primary combatants. Since 1948, the nations of the world have been "choosing up sides" in the crisis between Palestinians and Jews. In many instances, the foreign policy of many nations is not only inconsistent but hypocritical. This is well illustrated by the French government who have repeatedly supported the sale of every conceivable weapon and armament within their military arsenal to Israel. At the same time, they have been quietly furnishing the raw materials and technological expertise to the Arab nation of Iraq, enabling the Iraquis to be one of the first Arab nations to develop nuclear energy. Similar policies are carried out by West Germany, Great Britain, South Africa and a host of South American countries. Double-dealing has become the status-quo, the norm of conventional diplomacy. But the day is fast approaching when hard-fast decisions will be demanded by the two major parties from their "allies." Each nation in the world community will be called upon to declare its allegiance, perhaps to the extent of military commitment of their own national troops and/or weapons. The progenitor of such an open policy of political alignment is none other than one we might correctly title, "Ambassador Oil." Though every nation is in some way affected by this "ambassador," the two nations who will benefit most, by loss or gain, are the United States and the Soviet Union. Both countries project a long range need for importing oil and other important fuels for their energy consuming societies.

Thus the lines are drawn for what must become the final act in the determination of the Arab/Israeli scenario. In truth, the outcome will depend greatly upon the actions and attitudes of the following three antagonists:

(A) Palestinian Arabs Vs. Israeli Jews

    (B) All other Arabs   Vs. All other Jews

    (C) The U.S.S.R.   Vs. The U.S.A.

Despite the immense economic and political investments of both the United States and Russia, and despite any of a number of political ramifications affecting one or the other in the case of some type of settlement, the principle parties to be considered are the first pairing, for it is they who must be satisfied. It is they who must live as neighbors, either in peace or war; and it is they who will continue to be happy or displeased depending on the nature of the solution. And it is time for all interested nations to unite in a consensus of concern for the two parties, and cease the political "gamesmanship" of utilizing both the opponents and the conflict for personal gain. If we seriously seek an end to this turmoil we must begin the search for peace with a search for a workable formula which will establish the normal, healthy human relations between Palestinian Arabs and Israeli Jews, and we recognize they appear mutually exclusive of one another. Yet, no one can be certain this is the case, for NO ONE HAS EVER APPROACHED THE SUBJECT IN AN OBJECTIVE AND UNBIASED ATTITUDE! This includes representatives of Arabs and the Jews. What has taken place thus far has been theatrical oratory, intimidation tactics, and mass media manipulation for propaganda with which to affect world opinion. Mr. Begin continues the now familiar refrain that "we will never return one inch of occupied territory or the West Bank lands" declaring that to do so would somehow precipitate another "Holocaust." Meanwhile, militant Arab leaders vow to "drive the Jews into the sea" before agreeing to any settlement or peace proposal. Inasmuch as we have insisted that the first step of any serious effort to attain a settlement is to reinstitute human relations among and between the parties, I wish to suggest some basic principles which might serve to govern relations between Palestinian Arabs and Israeli Jews. These principles, if expressed and somehow accepted by both sides through intensive negotiation and conciliation, could then become the very Cornerstone of an acceptable solution to all concerned.

The Principles:

(A) No Israeli citizen now living in Israel will be subjected now or in the future to any personal harm or injury, nor will the solution foster material harm to their possessions.

(B) Likewise, no Palestinian Arab who lived in Palestine in 1948 will be subjected now or in the future to any personal harm or injury, nor will the solution cause material harm to their possessions. This principle must naturally apply to descendants of these Palestinian Arabs.

(C) Both Palestinian Arabs and Israeli Jews will be permitted to live under the administrative and/or political organizations that prove mutually acceptable to both groups.

To many these principles may seem simplistic or casual, but as I have stated, they are (or could be) the beginning of the pavement on the road to peace. But no road is completed without careful deliberation, a well-defined blueprint, and leadership that views the successful completion of their project as an honorable and necessary goal. The encountering of occasional boulders in road-building is not at all unusual and is to be expected. So it is we encounter several "boulders" which must first be removed if construction is to begin.

1. The first obstacle to the implementation of the three principles is the situation of a returning Palestinian Arab who returns to find his former home, land, and property are now owned and occupied by an Israeli Jew. Suppose his farmland now belongs to a "Kibutz" or communal Israeli farm? How will this conflict be resolved? Is there a willingness on the part of the Israelis to even discuss what would be a fair and equitable settlement? Will the Palestinian endeavor to deal realistically with alternative solutions, including the resettlement of Israeli citizens, land value, etc?

2. A second obstacle would comprise the establishment of an administrative and/or political organization which would be acceptable by both parties. The current Israeli leaders have said "no" to any consideration of an autonomous

Palestinian state within or adjacent to Israeli borders or territory, although Begin is fond of using the term "Autonomy Talks" whenever it is politically advantageous to do so. But he does express the real fears and questions of many Israeli people as to the form of government which might evolve from such a consideration. How independent would the Arab government be of Israeli law and jurisdiction?

Would the resultant government become a bi-national state? Or would there be a resumption of two separate, sovereign states living side by side? It seems certain that no Palestinian Arab is willing to accept Israeli law and military presence in his own city or state. Likewise, it is doubtful that the Israelis will permit an armed Arab state to function as a fully independent nation with jurisdiction and authority over Israeli citizens.

Despite the gravity of the disputed issues just mentioned, I do believe these too can be overcome *IF THOSE THREE PRINCIPLES OUTLINED PREVIOUSLY HAVE BEEN FULLY AND GENUINELY ACCEPTED BY BOTH SIDES!* Without such a general and unconditional acceptance there is no hope of any injustice, whether Arab or Jew, being fairly redressed. And without proper redress, there will be no peaceful solutions forthcoming.

Before the important principles can be accepted and thus usher in some form of normalized relations from which serious dialogue can begin, another serious "boulder" must be removed. The Palestinians are the Arabs most directly involved in the conflict and not their Arab neighbors, sympathetic though they may be. Therefore, the Palestinian people must first have an officially recognized spokesman to enter into the discussions and considerations. It is now clear to the vast majority of the world that the Palestine Liberation Organization is indeed the body chosen to represent the people and their plight. There simply are no other viable alternate spokesmen who carry the unqualified support and endorsement of the Palestinian people.

The Israeli government has maintained a hard line against any dialogue or discussion with the Palestine Liberation Organization declaring the organization to be a "band of terrorists" who murder innocent men, women and children.

But as we have already learned from Chapter 2, terror, murder, assassination and atrocities have occurred on BOTH SIDES since the beginning of the conflict. Bombings of Arab homes, automobiles and business establishments, as well as numerous assassinations of Arab and PLO officials such as the former PLO chief of intelligence, Ali Hassan Salameh. He was killed by a remote-controlled bomb in Beirut in 1979. Most informed sources concluded the bombing to be the work of Israel's own intelligence agency or Mossad. Again, our study in Chapter 4 revealed the inner workings of the many Jewish Terrorist groups who murder innocent men, women and children. For Israel to declare the PLO to be only a terrorist organization, and not comprising any political or governmental structure representative of the Palestinian Arabs is unfounded. The PLO is the only real Palestinian representation for the displaced Palestinian Arabs. There can be no dialogue or serious peace proposals without the inclusion of the PLO. Many American diplomats in the Middle East maintain that no peace is possible without their participation. In the words of Harold Saunders, former Assistant Secretary of State, "It is not possible to get support for a settlement on the Israeli-occupied West Bank without the PLO." Mr. Saunders served under President Carter. In a news release (7/5/81) it was learned that the United States has conducted serious talks with the PLO for at least seven years. These talks were carried out with the full knowledge and approval of Presidents Nixon, Ford, Carter and Reagan. Despite public pronouncements emphasizing that any negotiations with the PLO are prohibited, these secret negotiations have been continuing in an effort to find some possible method or solution to the conflict. We will have more to say about the possibility of negotiation between the Israelis and the Palestinian Liberation Organization a bit later.

Israel itself, already fully organized, must be asked to express its willingness to enter into serious discussion with the organized representative of the Palestinian Arabs. Also, they must express a willingness to accept the three major principles we set forth earlier. These are not as specific as the decisions of the United Nations in 1967 and 1973, which have been all but ignored and refused by Israel. If these more general principles relating to humanitarian treatment and recognition can be accepted by both sides, then it is possible that a real foundation may be laid upon which a peace proposal can be erected.

But I am convinced no progress will take place towards a true and lasting peace until the Israeli leaders first ADMIT THEY HAVE PERPETRATED A GREAT WRONG AND INJUS- TICE AGAINST AN INNOCENT PEOPLE! Until such an honest admission is verbalized without qualification, the Arab repre- sentatives will never agree to any deliberations. And until then, the world will continue to hear the same tired, and over- used "reasons" why Israel's "Theft of a Nation" is really justified and correct, and should be supported by all the nations of of the world. It is doubtful that the present govern- ment leaders of Israel will ever "admit" such injustice unless political pressure is applied from the long-time allies and supporters of the Jewish State. This is especially true of the United States and President Reagan. The naivete of past Presi- dents and Congressional leaders of the United States must be replaced with an attitude of objective reality, and the courage to express publicly our position relative to Israel and the Palestinian issue. The entire conflict MUST BE REMOVED FROM THE "GAME BAG" OF THE POLITICIANS AND NATIONAL LEADERS! Policy, attitudes and applied diplom- acy must, at long last, be formulated on the basis of truth rather than the influence of a powerful lobby, or threat of the loss of support to win or maintain a political position. In other words, it will take men and women DEDICATED TO TRUTH AND JUSTICE; men and women, political leaders, who are more concerned with moral right than pragmatic wrong; true public servants who place more emphasis on world peace achieved through justice than re-election to a pompous politi- cal position devoid of basic human compassion and concern for the deceived and victimized people of the world.

Likewise, the world's political leaders will not seek nor possess such a thirst for justice unless and until their citizens demand such attitudes and actions. And this demand cannot be made by the citizens until they are informed of the total history and verifiable truths which comprise the Middle East conflict. It is just such an awareness that prompted the author to write this present manuscript. Now until the world is informed and apprised of the facts, and demands a just and equitable settlement, the Zionist leaders will continue to seek international support and legitimization of their illegitimate state. They have become past masters in the use of propaganda and media control which always portrays them as "poor little Israel," the "David" of the Middle East who must stand and fight against the "Goliath" of the Arab nations. The most frequently heard "reasons" propagated over the past thirty-three years which attempt to justify their seizure and military occupation of another people and their country, are the following:

(1) THE PREVENTON OF ANOTHER JEWISH HOLO-CAUST.

(2) AN ISRAELI STATE IS THE ONLY BUFFER AGAINST RUSSIAN AND COMMUNIST INFILTRATION AND INFLUENCE IN THE MIDDLE EAST.

(3) THEY (JEWS) HAVE MADE PALESTINE INTO A FER-TILE FARMING COUNTRY INSTEAD OF THE DIS-MAL, BARREN WASTELAND IT ONCE WAS UNDER ARAB RULE AND OVERSIGHT.

(4) THE PARTITION OF PALESTINE WHEN COMPARED TO PARTITION OF OTHER COUNTRIES IS, SOME-HOW, JUST AND "SPECIAL."

I have already discussed the false concept that Israel is a tiny, outnumbered, precariously vulnerable nation surrounded by hordes of savage, barbarous Arab fanatics. One need only consult the numerous reports contained in the Congressional Record, or a multitude of books, some even written by native Jewish leaders such as "Battle For Peace" by Ezer Weizman, in order to learn that the military forces of Israel are second only to those of Russia and the United States. In point of fact, no other nation on earth has such a "standing army" and military machine capable of inflicting incalculable devastation against any adversary, as the military forces of Israel are capable of doing. Their principle antagonists, the Palestinian Arabs, are by comparison militarily impoverished and absolutely incapable of launching even the smallest of any conceivable "invasion" of powerful Israel. This is clearly evidenced by the terrible bombing raids carried out by waves of U.S. made phantom jets against "suspected" PLO headquarter buildings and refugee camps in southern Lebanon and the capital city of Beirut. These attacks continue at this writing (July, 1982) and are daily responsible for the death of hundreds of innocent women and children civilians. Surely such indiscriminate acts would necessitate immediate military response from the victims of such hostilities, but no military response is forthcoming, for the Palestinian people do not possess the conventional military arms or superbly trained army to initiate a successful military response. If, as is claimed by Israel, the PLO possessed the superior Russian arms and equipment which threatens the very existence of the Israeli state, then surely a full scale effort would be mounted to avenge the many victims of Israeli bombing attacks. There is no response because there is no "enemy" army to represent the Palestinians. Thus the well publicized "myth" of "tiny Israel" holding out against a giant Arab army is fully exploded and hopefully laid to rest.

But what of the claim that Israel must maintain control of Palestine in order to avoid another "holocaust"? This is perhaps the most despicable but effective excuse given by Israeli leaders, more especially Menachem Begin, for their continuing aggression against the Palestinians. Begin has repeatedly attempted to justify every hostile act by evoking memories of the Nazi Holocaust of World War II.

HOLOCAUSTOMANIA

"The recent Israeli attack on the Iraqi nuclear reactor and Israel's solid defense of its action clearly bear witness to the Begin government's lack of good faith in its dealings with other nations. When Prime Minister Begin JUSTIFIES THIS ATTACK BY EVOKING MEMORIES OF THE NAZI HOLOCAUST DURING WORLD WAR II, he and his government are certainly acting in bad faith."

"The Israeli Air Force attack on the 70-Megawatt nuclear reactor represents none other than a willful act of terror-

The Search for Peace / 121

ism on the part of the Begin government." (Congressional Record 6/11/81).

Thus spoke the Honorable Daniel K. Akaka, U.S. representative from the state of Hawaii. His statement is reflective of numerous congressional leaders and senior statesmen when they, along with the rest of a shocked and dismayed world, learned of the June 7, 1981, bombing attack upon the Arab nation of Iraq. Though Begin and the "hawks" of his cabinet at first claimed the reactor was nearly capable of producing atomic weapons to be used against Israel and attempted to use this as an excuse for the bombing, the world soon learned that the entire scenario was fabrication from start to finish. The reactor was many years from acquiring production of nuclear components for nuclear weaponry. There was no "secret reactor" buried under the existing reactor as was claimed by Begin. Once again, America had supplied the planes, bombs, and technological training enabling the Israelis to attack a sovereign, independent state and nation. Once again America and the other naive nations were to accept the explanation of an intentional terroristic act to be necessary for "proper defense of Israel." But this time there would be no "white wash" or media exoneration; for this time the United States would face the full backlash of Israel's action and like an overprotective parent who has for too long placated the unruly and undisciplined behavior of an only child and blindly tolerated intolerable attitudes and actions, the United States was placed in the embarrassing position of accepting responsibility for the Israeli attack or join the rest of the world nations in condemning them. Thus, for the first time in its history, the world body of the United Nations Security Council unanimously voted to condemn Israeli's raid, including the United States! This vote may serve to be the first feeble step taken by the United States and its political leaders to prove to those who have long maintained the U.S. practiced a "two-handed" policy of open support for all Israeli endeavors and opposition to Palestinian Arabs, that there is indeed some measure of concern for truth and justice in the Middle East Conflict.

THE POLITICAL HOLOCAUST

It is indeed puzzling to study the collective attitude of the European Jews who endured the many inhumane and barbaric acts of Nazi Germany during World War II, with the collective attitude of the Jewish Population of the 1980's. Despite the torture chambers, concentration camps and crematories, Jewish survivors and leaders repeatedly expressed their determination to retain their dignity. In 1945, while the gas chambers were still working, the greatest Judaic theologian of this century, Abraham Joshua Heschel, said:

"Our life is beset with difficulties, yet it is never devoid of meaning. . . . Our existence is not in vain. There is a Divine earnestness about our life. This is our dignity. To be vested with dignity means to represent something more than oneself."

". . . The time for the kingdom may be far off, but the task is plain; to retain our share in God in spite of peril and contempt."

In this simple affirmation of life in the face of death and defiance of despair, Heschel illustrated the spirituality of Judaism. He felt the atrocities were contributive to Jewish awareness:

". . . in this period our people attained the highest degree of inwardness. . . it was the golden period in the history of the Jewish soul."

One must question how the present-day Jews have come from that defiance of despair, from that affirmation of God's rule on earth and in heaven, to "the Holocaust"? How account for such a stark contrast between the dignity and hopefulness of Heschel who had personally suffered the loss of his entire family, and the bathos and obsession of those who, 36 years later, speak of nothing but transports, gas chambers, a million abandoned teddy bears, and the death of God? We find no expression of condemnation or "collective guilt" against the German people, Christians, or the world at large. Heschel knew that judgment belongs to God. Heschel mourned the events, but went on to other things. He is best remembered for writing more about Job than "Auschwitz."

During the 1950's there was a return to the synagogue among the American Jews. The sociologist Nathan Glazer wrote his book describing American Judaism without making more than passing reference to the war atrocities. Most Jewish communities were busy building for the future and were taking important leadership positions in both the political and industrial fields of post-war America.

Enter the striking contrast of the 1970's. Suddenly there is no way for one to address the Jewish world without referring to the "Holocaust." Today (1980's) there exists, without exaggeration, an "obsession" and preoccupation with the Holocaust in an effort to make the tragedy into the primary topic of discussion among Jews and Judaism. Serious consideration is being given to the proposal to set up "Holocaust centers" in every Jewish community. The centers would function like synagogues, comprised of buildings, professional staffs, exhibitions, programs and commemorative events.

Add to this obsession the President's Holocaust Commission formed under former President Carter in 1979, and the solemn candlelight memorial services held in the rotunda of the nation's Capitol for the past two years, and it becomes evident that this tragic event has become the most politicized and propagandized occurrence of recent memory. Who can doubt the aggrandizement attained by the Israeli State with the political leaders of America as television networks dutifully filmed and replayed for millions of viewers in prime evening time a tearful President Reagan, after hearing the retelling of familiar horror stories, addressing the Jewish leaders with trembling voice reduced to a whisper and assuring them (and the present-day Israeli state) of America's unfeigned and continued support? Not surprisingly, one finds many American Jews are puzzled at both the "commemorative" services and the Holocaust Commission. As American citizens, they wonder why there has not been a commission created to memorialize the Armenian massacres of World War I, or the political violence and mass murder of over TWENTY MILLION RUSSIANS AND CHINESE CITIZENS during the bloody regimes of communist's Stalin and Chairman Mao? And where is the commission dedicated to the slaughter of untold millions of Poles, Slovaks, Russians and countless other nationalities and cultures obliterated by the Germans during World War II? And If, indeed, we are justified in establishing adequate commissions and memorials to innocent peoples and cultures, where is the long overdue Presidential Commission to commemorate the gennocidal annihilation of our own American Indians? Surely there is justifiable perplexity by many who fail to comprehend the "deep concern" of political leaders over acts committed abroad, when these same atrocities occur in one's own homeland and they are conveniently forgotten.

The "Holocaust" has become a powerful, evocative symbol primarily through the efforts of theologian Emil Fackenheim. Prior to the 1967 war, Fackenheim was known as a religious existentialist and somewhat of a scholar of Hegel. His work is dominated by the symbol: "Auschwitz." One of Fackenheim's critics, Michael Wyschogrod, declares that Fackenheim has substituted "the commanding voice of Auschwitz" for the revelation of Sinai, and Hitler for Moses. He is credited the apophthegm, "Let's not hand Hitler any more victories." The meaning of that statement is that Jews should practice Judaism, and Jews and gentiles should support the State of Israel. But such support MUST NOT BE FORTHCOMING AT THE COST OF JUSTICE AND DECEIT! In fact it was Richard L. Rubenstein, the Judaic theologian and "Holocaustian," who said:

> *"The most appropriate American memorial to the victims of the Holocaust ought to be a national effort for the understanding of large-scale political injustice and violence."*

And it is just such large-scale political injustice and violence which has been and continues to be inflicted against the Palestinian People.

WHAT SHOULD THE HOLOCAUST REALLY MEAN?

The Holocaust should be considered for what it was but more importantly, why it occurred. Although most of the post-war population of today relates the Holocaust to the

European Jews only, it must be remembered that the Jews were perhaps five million of over twenty million European civilians lost during the war. That such a travesty could occur in modern civilization is a tragic reminder of the boundless depravity and total insensitivity attainable by godless men and nations of our planet. It must cause us to examine closely any philosophy or hypothesis that suggests that one man or race is superior or inferior to another. Hitler believed and sought to apply the popular teaching of Darwinian evolution by creating the "super-race" of Nazi Germany, while at the same time assisting "nature" in the destruction of what he considered an inferior race, meaning the Jews.

Negatively, we must not permit self-serving politicians to manipulate and propagandize the Holocaust to the exclusion of political justice in Palestine. America and the world in general must not be blinded by sentiment, disabled in our judgment by the stories of concentration camps, torn Torahs, and cakes of soap made of the fat of Jewish bodies. If we are so incensed by these events, we must likewise accept and endure the everlasting shame of unspeakable acts of savagery initiated against the American Indians at such "forgettable" places as Washita River, Sand Creek, and Wounded Knee, including the fashioning of saddle horns, chaps and other clothing from the bodies of American Indians. Atrocity has no ethnic or geographical boundaries but exists wherever men and nations seek to impose an unjust and immoral rule and subjugation over others.

The Holocaust must not be permitted to be used to perpetrate similar or even greater injustices against Palestinian Arabs. The Palestinians feel they are being punished for what Nazi Germany did to the Jews. The world seems to be compensating the Jews for the evils of the Holocaust at the expense of the Arabs. THE INNOCENT PARTY IS PAYING FOR THE GUILT OF HITLER'S GERMANY! It is sadly ironic that the Jews who experienced such discrimination and homelessness should display such unjust treatment of another nation and people. Does not such an attitude in effect endorse the very principles of their own persecutors used against them during the war?

HOLOCAUST: 1. "a sacrifice consumed by fire." 2. "a

thorough destruction especially by fire." (Webster's New Collegiate Dict., 1981) A seemingly simple term by definition, but with a connotation of unparalleled pain and inhumanity. Which world-citizen would not agree with Menachem Begin's best known statement: "NO MORE HOLOCAUSTS?" Who is there who does not sympathize with those Jews who lost families and loved ones in the horror of war?

But let those come forward to be named who are willing to support the invasion, conquest by force of arms, and total military occupation of an innocent and independent country, all because of the activities and attitudes of a madman and his cohorts against an ethnic minority living in their own country. There can be no justification of past injustices by the establishing and continuation of current injustices against Palestinian Arabs. "NO MORE HOLOCAUSTS...NEVER AGAIN!" For Arabs and Jews alike.

The second most frequently used "reason" given by Israeli leaders and their supporters in order to justify the continued occupation of Palestine is: "An Israeli state is the only buffer against Russian and communist infiltration and influence in the Middle East." Again, we must recall our discussion of communism and the Middle East people in Chapter 4. We learned that the presence of communism is an accepted fact by the Israeli governing body, the Knesset or Parliament. An "official" and duly recognized party active in government affairs is the Communist party of Israel. In examining the record, we learned that the Russian Ambassador to the U.N. freely and openly supported Zionism in its early formation and later, its claim to Palestine. It is a fact that Zionism is a human ideology that even many atheists hold. Many reliable sources indicate that *LESS THAN TEN PERCENT OF ISRAELIS ARE ORTHODOX JEWS, AND MANY ARE NOT ONLY NOT RELIGIOUS, BUT ARE MILITANTLY ANTI-GOD!* The Palestinians have long stated that nothing would make the Middle East a center for communism except the success of Zionism in attaining their goals and objectives. One is hard pressed to find a comparable communist party representative entrenched within the infrastructure of an Arab country. The very nature of the Arab culture and religion would absolutely preclude any alliance with communism. Thus the claim that the Israeli state is a buffer against communism is not only untrue, but a very real contradiction. Communism and atheism, whether in Russia or Israel, are anti-God systems of thought and government which encourage nationalistic humanism (such as Zionism) while at the same time discouraging individual achievement and the pursuit of moral truth.

One should be cognizant of the fact that the majority of contemporary Zionists now residing in Israel are converts from other stock. The current military leaders and politicians in Israel are immigrants from Russia, Central America, and the United States. Most are of Khazar descent; Caucasian Russians converted to Judaism in the eighth century by Byzantine Jews. I once asked a group of young Israeli college students if they felt God had "returned" the promised land to them and their people. Their answer reflects a prevalent attitude among present-day Israeli citizens. First of all, they resented any implication that "God" had done anything for them: "We are gods," they said, "and we will fulfill the prophecies the way we wish by the power of the Uzzi" (an Israeli submachine gun used by Israeli military and sold worldwide by Israel). This same group stated their disgust with tourists (including Jewish tourists) from other countries who tour Palestine expecting to find a nation of "believers" and "Law keepers." Few outside Israel are aware of the bitter hatred and in-fighting which continues among the orthodox "Gush Emunim," the "Hassidim," the "Kach" and nonreligious citizens. This hostility will become familiar to the outside world shortly as Menachem Begin attempts to initiate the many "promises" he made to the Jewish minority parties which enabled him to win the office of Prime Minister for a second term in 1981. Begin agreed Israel would annex occupied Arab lands in Gaza and the West Bank of Jordan, even after granting the Palestinians currently residing in those areas so-called "self-rule" for a five year period. In other words, no matter what is agreed upon in any future peace talks or diplomatic efforts to achieve a lasting peace, the Palestinians can look forward to only five years of limited independence before their homes, lands and businesses are once again "taken" from them. For further consideration of the extremist attitude and actions of the religious parties of

Israel, review Chapter 4.

Other concessions by Begin to the religious minority parties will include the banning of Israeli airline flights on the Jewish Sabbath (which El Al officials claim will cost them an added $10,000,000 loss), higher wages for rabbis from an already strapped national budget, a halt to all public transportation on the Sabbath, as well as continued expansionism through the establishment of more illegal settlements on Palestinian land illegally "confiscated" under the guise of "national defense." Although 60 percent of the meat consumed by Israeli's consists of pork products, Begin has promised to eliminate all pork, as well as enforce the strict and minute dietary laws. All of these acts will serve to spark riots and internal strife on an unprecedented scale. This situation could well be a political time bomb which threatens not only Israeli stability, but more especially, any possibility for real peace efforts on the part of the Palestinian People and interested Western Nations and their leaders.

By close examination of the political and pragmatic philosophy of the majority of Israeli citizens, the Israeli state cannot be said to be the only buffer against Russian or communist infiltration of the Middle East. Whenever political policy is determined by popularity and political "deals" rather than principle and the pursuit of truth, when the attitudes and activities of any nation are determined by the minority of that nation on the basis of political collusion, then that nation is dangerously close to transcending the role of a "buffer" to that of a "conduit" for whatever philosophy which might be supportive of that self same government.

The third "reason" given for the continued occupation is:

"They (the Jews) have made Palestine into a fertile farming country instead of the dismal, barren wasteland it once was under Arab rule."

Having studied and excavated in Palestine as well as conducting tours of the Middle East for ten years, I can speak firsthand concerning this third point. American Christians by the hundreds of thousands pour into the Holy Land on tours that, although sponsored by Christian organizations in this country, are arranged largely by Israeli tourist agencies. No opportunity is missed by these agencies to promote the Zionist mythology of a "homeland" for persecuted, God-fearing and obedient Old Testament Jews, which the majority of the Israeli citizenry soundly denies and rejects as false. Instead of being shown the numerous Christian sites, shrines and locations, they are shown the Shrine of the Book where the Dead Sea Scrolls are kept, the Hadassah Hospital with the Chagall windows, the Hebrew University, the Herzl Museum, and of course, the Yad Vashem momument which perpetuates the memory of Jewish victims of World War II. A cursory tour of the major Christian sites may be taken, but the emphasis is on the state of Israel. I have taken numerous people to Israel on one of my own tours who had previously been on one of these Israeli tours. They consistently spoke of the "indoctrination" they received as well as the lack of historical and biblical sites they had not been shown. Perhaps the best propaganda site is the journey to northern Galilee and the plains of Sharon known as the heartland and breadbasket of Israel. As the tour bus stops on a high hill overlooking the rich and fertile valley, the tourists are informed that these plains were once arid and deserted, and have "come to life" only since the area came under Israeli control and cultivation. The tourists are then invited to look with obvious dismay at the barren hills of Moab which the Arabs have failed to bring to life. The "evidence" seems conclusive; Israel "deserves" the land. Some ignorant evangelical "pastors," totally devoid of any knowledge of the history and circumstance of Palestine, attempt to account for the dramatic differences between Israeli and Arab lands as being a special intervention by God on behalf of the Jews. As I discussed in the prophecy chapter (5) they mistakenly imply that the occupation of Palestine by foreign Jews is fulfilling the prophecy of the Old Testament and the fertile fields are proof of that fulfillment. Many "duped" Christians believe the entire desert regions of Israel are "blooming and giving forth fruit" when, in fact, the Negev and Judean areas remain as they have always been, barren and empty!

The tourists are not told that the plains of Sharon and the Galilee have always been the choice land, fruitful for thousands of years. The Jaffa oranges were cultivated by Arabs who never had the millions of dollars in foreign aid that Israel now enjoys. These Jaffa and Jericho oranges are known round the world as the most succulent and delicious fruit available.

The tourists are likewise not told that these fruitful sections of land were portioned out to Israel back in 1948. Nor are they aware of the thousands of acres of olive groves and vineyards which have dried up for lack of Israeli knowledge or inclination to preserve what had been cultivated and terraced by Arabs with wooden plows and donkeys since before the time of Christ. If one studies the population displacement of Arabs and Jews within Palestine, one will quickly discover that the majority of farmers and laborers who occupy and work these rich fields of Israel are Arabs! The only thing that has really changed in the past few thousand years is the ownership of these fields and orchards as a result of the illegal conquest and continued occupation by Israel. The farming skills and know-how is still supplied by the indigenous Arabs.

The fourth "reason" for the Israeli occupation is:

"The partition of Palestine, when compared to partitions of other countries, is, somehow, just and special."

In the Atlantic Monthly of January 1969, an article appeared written by a Mr. Charles Yost who was ultimately appointed chief representative of the United States to the U.N. In this article, Mr. Yost seems to desire to appear objective but he repeats those same tired statements used to confuse the real issues of Palestine, and which continue to block any real efforts to obtain a solution to the Palestinian problem.

In a vain attempt to show the relative insignificance of claimed injustices by the Palestinians, Yost says:

"What most needs recognition is, of course, the realities. There are many international situations in this day and age which are of debatable justice; partitioned Germany..."

Yost, like many others before him, attempts to reduce the gravity of the "Theft of a Nation." His illogical premise is this: since the partitioning of Nazi Germany was unjust and exists today no one should object to the fact that a deliberate injustice has been carried out elsewhere in the world. One is hard pressed to understand or correlate the logic or ethic of his argument. In fact, I see no resemblance between post-war Germany and occupied Palestine whatsoever! The historical causes and events which led to the partitioning of the militant and aggressive Germany and those which subjected the innocent Palestinians to such severe injustice, beginning with the Balfour Declaration of 1917, have absolutely no relationship at all. Partitioning of both countries and peoples is wrong! But if we were to compare the two partitioned peoples, we would find that the German citizens on both sides generally remained in their own houses on their own lands. But the Palestinians lands and houses were and are occupied by foreign Jews and those Palestinians who remained in their country are subject to the governing of a totally foreign government.

Mr. Yost said he desired to recognize "realities." The reality of the Palestinian issue is that a great injustice has been carried out against an innocent people, and these many injustices continue to fester within the hearts and minds of the victims and must of necessity one day give way to a massive explosion which will then usher in the "reality" of justice and retribution. This reality must be recognized by all politicians, statesmen, governments and societies and action must be taken to alleviate existing injustices if the damage from the forthcoming explosion is to be limited and restricted to the less degree possible.

You will recall that we listed three sets of principle antagonists, including Palestinian Arabs Vs. Israeli Jews. Thus far in our search for peace, we have examined the possibility of peace through diplomacy and the possible definitions of justice according to Arabs and Jews. I cannot stress enough the need for world communities to encourage these two primary adversaries to attempt a beginning dialogue with the objective of settling their long-lived dispute. This is easier said than done. The major world powers continue to connive and manipulate one side or the other for their own selfish political aspirations and until they exert their utmost influence in an effort to bring the Arab and Jew to a position of discussion, I see no possibility for any peace in the Middle East, and the answer is NO, PEACE IS NOT OBTAINABLE THROUGH DIPLOMACY!

Two other "antagonists" or sometimes, as is the case, "protagonists," are: All other Arabs Vs. All other Jews. Let's first examine the relationship between the Palestinian Arabs and Arabs "in general." This relationship is not at all like that which exists between Jews in general and Israeli Jews. The Arab countries support the Palestinians for several main reasons which warrant our investigation.

(1) First of all, Arab leaders and their people really believe that "right makes right" and right is on the side of the Palestinians. They believe the historical facts are quite clear and serve to indict the Zionist Israeli state. To them it is a clear case of a foreign invasion by a foreign people, with the subsequent military conquest by force of arms in collusion with voracious political aspirations of unprincipled and immoral European politicians. The collective Arab nations have waited for a collective world justice to attend the dispute, but no such justice has thus far appeared. Today, instead of continuing their centuries old wars and disputes with one another, they have recently been solidified for the first time in many centuries by their determination to see the Palestinian Arabs returned to their homeland. To the Arab mind and way of thinking, there is no compromise for truth and right, justice and retribution.

The Arabs also see the Israeli biblical claim as patently false. They point to the Old Testament story of Abraham and Ishmael, Esau and Jacob as evidence of their "right" to dwell in the "promised land." They correctly point out to negligent evangelical "literalists" the clear warnings and pronouncements of doom and desolation against the Jews for breaking their covenant with God.

(2) A second reason the other Arab nations support the cause of the Palestinian Arabs is simple: they are blood relatives. It becomes a case of someone picking on another's little brother; "If you fight with him, you're going to be fighting both of us, for we are family." With modern air travel and technologies shrinking the vast geographic distances between peoples and nations, and the ongoing emphasis of ethnocentrism, the Arab people at large have begun drawing together

for both cultural identity and mutual protection. They have discovered they too can implement change on the political status quo by utilizing the world hunger for oil as an incentive for their being considered in the many important political problems of the day, including the Palestinian issue. Prince Faisal was fond of saying, "We are not one but many; we are not the only Arabs, but we are Arabs only."

(3) A third reason the Palestinian Arabs have unanimous support from the rest of the Arab world is due to their religious relationship. Nearly all of the Palestinians, like most of their Arab brothers, are Muslims. Now if blood is thicker than water, then religion is the central binding element of mankind. In Chapter 3, we considered the religion of Islam and noted its deep emphasis upon personal devotion to God and the brotherhood of "the faithful." It was the "Jihaad" or "holy wars" which accounted for the immediate spread of Islam in the seventh century, and it is this same religious fervor present among the Arab nation which draws them together as one nation and one people.

(4) A fourth reason for Arab support of the Palestinians is the fact that nearly all Arab leaders consider the Zionist state of Israel a very real threat to all Arabs and their countries. They envision the insatiable imperialism of the Zionist leaders driving them on to further conquests and subjugation of Arab peoples and nations.

> Imperialism: *"The policy, practice, or advocacy of extending the power and dominion of a nation, especially by direct territorial acquisition or by gaining indirect control over the political or economic life of other areas."* (Webster's New Collegiate Dictionary, 1981)

The invasion and conquest of Palestine by the foreign Zionists most certainly lends some credence to both the definition of imperialism and the fears of the Arab people. This fear is well illustrated by a recent archaeological find in Syria. Tell Mardikh or Ebla was the object of excavation for the University of Rome since 1964. In 1978 it was revealed that among the thousands of tablets found preserved at the massive site and dating from 2400 B.C. were accounts of trade conducted with cities mentioned in the biblical narratives including Sodom and the other four cities of the plain. According to the original epigrapher, Professor Pettinato, various biblical personal names appear among the tablets, including biblical accounts of the special creation and the "Kings list" of Genesis 14. But the crucial question is that of the language of the Ebla community. It was originally announced that it was definitely a very early dialect of Semitic origin. Enter the Arab concern over Zionist imperialism, and we now have a raging battle between the original epigrapher who was "relieved" of his duties, along with other outstanding language scholars who accepted his readings, against the Syrian government and the more liberal "scholars." The real issue is the language being admitted to be of ancient Hebrew or Semitic origin, for the Syrians (Arabs) think that the Jews will "lay claim" to their northern country as they have done in Palestine; "We were once there, our ancestors ruled, owned and lived in that place, therefore it belongs to us today."

How very sad it is to observe the revolting presence of politics intruding into the scientific realm of archaeology. But we can see from this one illustration the ramifications of the Arab's concern for the thirst of political Zionism. I must state that I know of no desire on the part of any Arab nation or people outside of Palestine to exploit the issue or the country for any private or personal benefit. In point of fact, the oil-rich countries such as Saudi Arabia, Iraq, Sudan and the rest have literally nothing to gain by their unswervable support of the displaced Palestinian People.

For the first time in the history of the Arab people, they are united around the single goal of assisting the Palestinians in their quest for justice. The many facets of the Palestinian movement are obviously funded by their fellow Arab states and leaders. American politicians who are fond of being known as "friends of Israel" are quick to point out that many Arab countries oppose Israel and are merely using the Palestinians and their cause for their own gain. But this is absolutely false! The only true statement is that ALL THE ARAB NATIONS AND PEOPLE OPPOSE THE EXISTING STATE OF ZIONIST ISRAEL! They consider it immoral and illegal, and must of necessity be dealt with in a realistic manner.

(5) A fifth and final reason for the Arab alliance is geographical. Four Arab states are the immediate neighbors of Palestine. One of these, Jordan, had formed one single state with that part of Palestine (Old Jerusalem) which had not been occupied by Israel prior to 1967.

WHY OTHER JEWS SUPPORT THE ISRAELI JEWS AND STATE

(1) Worldwide Jewish support is directly linked to Zionist objectives of establishing a Jewish state in which every Jew in the world has the right to settle. We examined the origins of the Zionist movement including its motivation, proponents, etc. in Chapter 3. The state of Israel provides the literal fulfillment of the Zionist declaration for a Jewish homeland. Also, it is thought of as a place of refuge or safety to which Jews can escape from any future persecutions similar to those occurring in Western European countries during the early nineteenth century.

(2) A second reason for Jewish support is that the continued existence of a Jewish state satisfies the inner longing of many Jews for a Jewish national homeland which, they imagine, gives them a formal voice in international affairs. Indeed, there is no other such "religious state" which can compare with Israel today. No other ethnic or religious group can claim their own "state" and homeland and exercise full diplomatic recognition in all the world councils and organizations.

(3) A third reason "outside" Jews support the Zionist state is financial pragmatism: Israel can be used as a means for foreign investments from around the world. Jewish capital from around the world is heavily invested in the ongoing state of Israel, and in some cases these investments may be questionable as to whether they are made for the benefit of the country or the investor.

(4) Many orthodox Jews (most living in the U.S.) support the Israeli state because of mistaken interpretations and teachings about the Abrahamic Covenant and various biblical prophecies concerning Israel. Chapter 5 presented an indepth examination of this area of thought. From our study in

Chapter 5, we concluded that any who attempt to "force" the biblical text and/or prophecies to somehow support the establishment of the current Israeli state, be they Jews or Gentiles, they are absolutely wrong! God does not support, direct, or implement injustice, illegality, and deceit!

In an effort to be objective and fair, I will include several explanations as to why I cannot list the same reasons given for the Jewish supporters of Israel as those given for the Arab supporters of the Palestinians.

The Arab people of the many Middle Eastern countries, although quite different in societal structures and activities, are yet singularly Arabic in racial origin, religious persuasion, and political philosophy. The same cannot be said of the many Jews spread throughout the world. And here we find the answer to why the Israeli support from the other Jews is not the same as the Palestinian Arabs support from other Arabs. We know what the conditions and requirements are that cause one to be an Arab, but we do not know those same conditions and requirements which determine who is a Jew or what is "Jewishness." One Jewish intellectual was asked what he thought were the various "proofs" of being a Jew, and he replied: "Ask three Jews, get five opinions."

(1) Unlike the Arabs, Jewish people cannot claim racial or blood relationship. There are Jews in every anthropologically defined "race," from the black Ethiopian to the Chinese orthodox Jew. It was the madman Hitler who attempted to "purify" the Aryans by liquidating European Jews from Hungary, Poland, Germany, etc. There are black Jews, blue-eyed Jews, blond Jews among all the nations of the world. Surely no one would propose that any or all of them are "direct blood relatives" and descendants of Abraham, Isaac or David! Neither are they blood relatives of the immigrant Jews who have flooded into Palestine since 1948. More than 70 nations are represented among the Israeli population. No one today can claim to be "Jewish" on the basis of inheritance or ancient blood lines.

(2) Unlike the Arabs, those Jews living outside of Israel do not support the Israeli state because all Jews share the same religious faith and fervor. As I have pointed out, probably

fewer than ten percent of Israelis can be considered "orthodox" and by far the majority are not religious at all. I realize
that most tourists believe the opposite is true when they view
the activities at the wailing wall or the festival celebrations on
the most "holy" Jewish days; but one must constantly
remember that while thousands or perhaps even hundreds of
thousands of Israeli citizens fill the courtyard at the wailing
wall, they represent but a fraction of the total population of
nearly three million citizens! Support of "eretz" Israel from a
religious perspective is, at best, a minor consideration.

(3) Support of the Israeli state is not attributable to the
mythological existence of a Jewish culture. While traveling
the entire length and breadth of Palestine, I have encountered
every conceivable "type" of Jewish citizen, from an Oriental
Jewess in her Arab dress, alongside a tour group of Jews from
the East Side of New York, next to a group of native-born
Jews or "Sabras." Although they were all in Israel at the same
time together, they were quite obviously years and miles
apart in their cultural identities. I. A. Abaddy wrote in the
Jewish Quarterly:

*"To seek the common denominator in terms of either
ritual or speech or outlook is bound to prove hopeless."*

(4) Unlike the Arab nations and people, being a Jew is not
relatable to an overall political philosophy or consensus. As
we have previously noted, Zionism is not a religious persuasion, but a political idea. Israel today is a political state, but
there are millions of Jews who are not Israelis. Likewise, there
are thousands of "Israelis" who are not Jews! Confusion of this
important distinction and reality is due to a great extent to the
ignorance of "Christian" and/or evangelical ministers,
teachers, missionaries, etc.

In Chapter 3 we examined Zionism and concluded that any
one who confuses it (Zionism) as religiously oriented rather
than a political and economical movement, or any who
equate the modern state of Israel with the "Israel of God" is in
great need of the simple historical facts surrounding the
founding of the Zionist "homeland."

THE U.S.S.R. VS. THE U.S.A.

Our third principle pairing which must be considered before any serious effort is taken towards a lasting peace and settlement of the Middle East issue is the role and relationship of the two world powers, Russia and the United States. In Chapter 4 we considered the involvement of these two countries and the political ramifications of that involvement. At this juncture we only wish to stress the importance of these two nations voluntarily removing themselves from the conflict in order to allow the principle parties to work out their own settlement. The United States is now attempting to establish new relationships with various Arab countries in the pursuit of America's own political aspirations and requirements.

Both Russia and the United States are beginning to recognize their struggle to gain the upper hand on one another must be carried out in other areas of the world arena, and the winning of friends and allies beyond the Middle East will transcend their obsession with manipulating the Arab/Israeli dispute. One cannot realistically expect a cessation of hostility between these two nations of such opposing political philosophies, but with the new interest and influence of the other Western European countries in the Palestinian Conflict, it is at least possible that both superpowers might begin to lessen their political power play in favor of more convenient opportunities to achieve political superiority. The truth is that neither Russia nor the United States are really wanted in any Middle Eastern Country other than the Russian "satellite" countries such as Libya, Syria, etc. Neither is trusted by Middle East Nations regarding motives and interests in the negotiation of an acceptable peace. As I have stated previously, the possibility of achieving an equitable settlement between and among all principle parties of the conflict will not be realized until dialogue begins, continues, and concludes between the State of Israel, the Palestinian Liberation Organization (PLO) and any other spokesman designated by either Israel or the Palestinian People. Russia and the United States must step aside while encouraging the two opponents to begin some type of earnest dialogue with one another. Of course the possibility of this occurring will require the immediate abandonment of protracted political activities by both superpowers accompanied by a sincere desire for peace and stability in the troubled Middle East.

PRIMARY PREREQUISITES FOR PEACE

If there is ever to be a lasting peace in the Middle East, the two principle opponents must begin serious negotiations, paying attention to the following items which I consider of paramount importance:

1. The State of Israel and its leaders must:

    a. Recognize and admit the injustice and wronging of Palestinian Arabs including all acts of aggression and occupation since 1948.

    b. Immediately cease all annexation of Arab lands and curtail any further Expansionism and new settlements or defense acquisitions.

    c. Express a willingness to negotiate the return of captured land portions of the West Bank and Gaza Strip to their rightful owners among those returning Palestinian Arabs and/or their descendents.

    d. Pledge to adhere to the Security Council Resolution 242 passed on November 22, 1967, as well as all other pertinent resolutions.

    e. Recognize the P.L.O. as Representative and Spokesman for the Palestinian Arabs and express willingness to negotiate with them.

    f. Openly support the Right of Self Determination by all Palestinian Arabs living in the Occupied West Bank and Gaza Strip.

(a) For any of points (b) through (f) to even be considered, point (a) must first become a reality. This seemingly minor point will require perhaps more courage on the part of the Israelis than even the remaining points. Admission of exploitation and forcible annexation of Arab lands and possessions will demonstrate to the Palestinians and the Arab world the seriousness of Israel's search for peace; it will vindicate known historical fact as presented in the preceding chapters of this book, and will help assure the world community of the unequivocal sincerity of Israel. Acceptance of responsibility for the many injustices inflicted upon the Palestinian People is the first meaningful step to real peace.

(b) Verbal admission of inflicting wrongs and injustices will be of little value if not accompanied by the *immediate cessation of any further "settlements" or annexation of Arab lands!* This policy has been the major progenitor of hate and revulsion not only among the Arab victims, but the entire world community, including the United States. Israeli alienation from the world community has been primarily attributable to this policy. Even the Camp David Accord has at its heart and center the cessation of expansionist attitudes and actions. *NO ONE, INCLUDING THE PALESTINIAN ARABS,* will begin to believe in an Israeli desire for peace unless and until this policy is abandoned once and for all.

(c) Admission of wrong and cessation of all expansionist activities will set the stage for legitimate negotiation for the return of those properties illegally seized from the Palestinian People and/or the restitution or compensation for those lands in the form of fair financial renumeration to the legitimate Arab owners or their descendents. To simply agree to "permit" those Palestinians driven from their homes and properties to return is not enough. Restitution/compensation must accompany any peace proposal involving the Palestinian People as both they and the world community view this point as essential in arriving at a just and lasting peace.

(d) Resolution 242 defined the framework for a peaceful settlement in the Middle East. The resolution stipulated that the establishment of a just and lasting peace should include the application of two principles: the withdrawal of Israeli armed forces from territories occupied in the recent conflict, and the termination of all claims or states of belligerency and respect for and acknowledgement of the sovereignty, territorial integrity and political independence of every State in the area and their right to live in peace within secure and recognized boundaries free from threats or acts of force. The resolution also affirmed the necessity for guaranteeing freedom of navigation through international waterways in the area, for achieving a just settlement of the refugee problems, and for guaranteeing the territorial inviolability and political independence of every State in the area, through measures including the establishment of a demilitarized zone.

Under this resolution, the Camp David Agreement makes possible the return of the Sinai to Egypt who was the legal "owner" of this territory prior to the 1967 military action between Israel and its Arab neighbors. Likewise then, a key discussion in any future talks with Palestinian Arabs must center around the disposition of the old city of Jerusalem which was, prior to 1967, totally occupied by Arabs and administered as part of the Western region of Jordan. If 242 is carried out, Israel will withdraw, at least its military apparatus, from the West Bank (which includes Jerusalem) and the Gaza Strip. Any refusal or failure to be willing to negotiate such a withdrawal will be viewed as a direct rejection and violation of Resolution 242 and will be unacceptable to all Arab parties. This same resolution will grant access of waterways to Israel as well as the controlling Arab nations thus affording some assurance to Israel of independent trade with its current allies as well as continued security of its borders by military surveillance. If this resolution is going to be accepted by the Israeli state, then it is essential that all talk of moving the Israeli capital from Tel Aviv to Old Jerusalem cease immediately. Political statements such as those made by Begin and the Defense Minister, Ariel Sharon and other "hawkish" political leaders that "we will never give up Jerusalem" must be silenced if a sincere desire for peace is forthcoming. I will discuss a possible settlement of the Jerusalem problem in a concluding segment at the close of this chapter.

(e) "We will never recognize the PLO in any manner whatsoever." The world is well aware of this statement of Menachem Begin and other politicians, including former U.S. Presidents and Congressional leaders. It is also aware of the public acceptance of the PLO by both former Presidents Jimmy Carter and Gerald Ford on October 7, 1981, when both men publicly called for the United States to implement direct dialogue with the PLO in order to advance peace initiatives in the Middle East. You will recall our discussion of the PLO in

Chapter 4. The PLO is already a political reality without Israeli recognition, and worldwide recognition continues to this day. If the present Israeli Prime Minister and cabinet are unwilling to recognize the PLO in order to begin meaningful dialogue, then perhaps all hope of any immediate peace must be reserved for their successors. But to await the emergence of a more flexible government is to risk the peril of increased hostilities among those countries and nations committed to a final settlement of this conflict. Time is against such an immense gamble. The Israeli state may inaugurate limited "peace" treaties with the few Arab states willing to enter such a liaison like Egypt, but they will never achieve a total, lasting peace without recognizing the PLO as sole spokesman for the Palestinian People and a genuine effort to engage them (the PLO) in direct dialogue over the substantive issues already expressed. The PLO now has embassies, ambassadors, UN observors, and various political representation throughout the world. The image once accepted by most, that of bloodthirsty terrorists bent on total annihilation of all Jews from the face of the planet, is for all practical purposes, dead and gone. As the plight and terrible injustice perpetrated against the Palestinian Arabs became known throughout the world, the PLO grew rapidly in credibility and soon became recognized by nearly all the major nations of the world as the sole voice and representative of the Palestinian people. There can be no settlement without them!

(f) If the Israeli leaders recognize and admit to the many injustices and inequities perpetrated against the Palestinians, and by recognizing UN Resolution 242 and halting all further annexation of Arab land and properties they express a willingness to enter into serious dialogue with the representative chosen by the Palestinians themselves (the PLO), then the final point of openly supporting the Right of Self Determination of all Palestinian Arabs living in the West Bank and Gaza Strip will naturally follow. The Israeli military must be withdrawn from Gaza and the West Bank thus truly allowing the Arab inhabitants to decide their own destiny. This point, like the preceding ones, must be real and meaningful as opposed to what is currently being "offered" by the Begin government. When one considers the restrictions and qualifications imposed by the Israelis in the "Camp David Accord," the self-determination is reduced to mere verbiage. Palestinian autonomy means precisely what the Dictionary infers:

"The quality or state of being self-governing, especially the right of self-government, a self-governing state, self-directing freedom and moral independence." Webster's New Collegiate Dictionary, '81

At the present time of this writing, the Israeli government has stated on numerous occasions that the settlements will remain even though they are illegally established on land not legally purchased, and the Israeli army will defend them. Such adamancy has increased since the selection of Ariel Sharon to become the new Minister of Defense. He was hand-picked by Menachem Begin. Sharon has long been an open advocate of total domination of all of Palestine proper by Zionist Israel. He has opposed the return of Arab lands and properties under any circumstances, and is unwilling to entertain the notion of disassembly of any illegal settlements.

The quest for Palestinian Autonomy cannot begin until these settlements are dismantled and the legal land owners, including the displaced Palestinians, are permitted to reclaim and rebuild their former homes and properties. Then, when the Israeli state has demonstrated a measure of good faith and reliability, and without any intimidation at the hands of the Israeli military presence already withdrawn, the Palestinians can begin the important process of selecting the government of their choice. That choice will be final and accepted by Israeli leaders who would initiate all necessary actions and measures to support the decision.

If there is to be a lasting peace in the Middle East, both parties must express and demonstrate a willingness to discuss their grievances. We have discussed in the preceding pages the six most important items which the Israeli state and its citizens must comprehend and actively seek to negotiate with regard to the Palestinian Arabs. Now likewise, there are certain absolute considerations which must be forthcoming on the part of the Palestinian People and their elective government.

2. The Palestinians/PLO and any and all other spokesmen must:

   a. Recognize that the Jews and the Israeli Zionist State has an inherent right to exist in peace and safety.

   b. Cease all caustic and inflammatory rhetoric including the promise to "annihilate" the citizens of the state of Israel. This includes the maxim to "drive the Jews into the sea."

   c. Immediately halt any and all military and guerilla activities against the Israeli state and citizenry, including those events and activities often designated by some as "terrorist" activities.

   d. PLO leaders must demonstrate to Israeli satisfaction their control over all other parties and factions within the Palestinian camp,

   e. Agree to an equitable coexisting government of their selection. Although totally autonomous, they will respect the rights, laws and sovereignty of the State of Israel.

   f. Agree to end any demand for a "national" army within their own agreed boundaries.

(a) Adherence to this primary point will do much to allay the common notion that once permitted within the old borders of Palestine, returning Arabs would attempt to exterminate all Jews and Israeli citizens. Idealism and wistfulness must give way to reality. It is not realistic for Palestinian Arabs to expect the current state of Israel, though illegally established in 1948, to conveniently "fold up" and depart to other countries or homelands. Like it or not, nearly thirty-five years of existence and recognition by nearly all the civilized countries of the world have established the current Israeli state as a valid entity. The modern-day world would not consent to the demand that the Israeli state disband and desist as a prerequisite for peace. Nor will there ever be a consortium of agreement among all the Arab states affirming such an actuality. If and when Israeli leaders begin to carry out the previously discussed items of implementation, including recognition of the right of returning Palestinians and all who live in what is now "occupied territory" to determine their own government structure and lifestyle, then Palestinians must reciprocate by allowing the many Israeli citizens the same opportunity of self-determination.

(b) Inflammatory rhetoric, including the vow to annihilate the Jews or drive them all into the sea, among other slogans, has probably done more damage to the Palestinian cause than all the military actions combined. A civilized world will not accept such rhetoric as valid. A significant indication that the Palestinian Liberation Organization does indeed have direct control over all its factions would be seen in the cessation of hostile threats and rhetoric. Words must be replaced with actions demonstrating the Palestinian desire to seek a real peace. Both parties must exchange verbal propaganda of the past, for tangible concessions for the future. Palestinian representatives must express their acknowledgement of the right of Israel and its people to co-exist.

(c) The "hard-liners" of the Israeli government will be silenced only when it has been clearly demonstrated to the world community that all military and guerilla activities have been halted. In pursuit of real and lasting peace, all hostile actions against Israel and its citizens must be completely stopped, without exception! Without the potential raids or threat of violent activities, the Israeli "hawks" will have lost their primary excuse for refusing to seek an equitable peace with the Palestinian people. Removal of possible attack and acts of aggression will also lend impetus to the real possibility of the removal of Israeli military forces from any and all returned lands and properties.

(d) Collectively speaking, if the three aforementioned items are initiated and clearly carried out, then it will be obvious to the world and the Israeli people that the Palestinian groups and their leaders have consolidated into one body and one voice. The PLO claim to be the only true voice of the Palestinian people will then be valid, and sincere negotiations and preliminary discussions can begin between the two bodies. This control of all members of the displaced Palestinians will not be easy to achieve, but is an absolute necessity. All non-primary parties and countries must voluntarily remove themselves from positions of decision making, including the United States and Russia, Syria, Iraq and all other supporters, whether they support Israel or the Palestinians. The Arab people in surrounding countries who have long stood with the alienated Palestinians must now step aside, disdaining any personal desires or attitudes in favor of permitting the Palestinian people to speak only for themselves, and themselves alone!

(e) If the Palestinian Arabs are to ever exercise a truly independent and autonomous government within what is now the West Bank and occupied territory, they (the Palestinians) must first agree to a preliminary co-existent government structure which would permit an independent Israeli state to exist alongside of an independent Palestinian state. The Arab world must not demand any less autonomy or independence for the Israeli state than they are seeking for the Palestinian people. To accomplish or establish such an attitude of "peaceful co-existence" will require those Palestinian leaders who, having already consolidated the authority and power of factional groups, to deal with this subject from a perspective of absolute reality. Reality dictates there can be no Israeli or Palestinian state without the co-existence of both.

(f) A final obstacle to a peaceful settlement of this conflict is the oft-repeated demand by many Arab nations (although not necessarily by Palestinians themselves) for a "national" army to be established within the boundaries of the Palestinian state. If negotiations make all the previous five points a reality, then there will be no reason or rationale for a "national Palestinian army." The Palestinian state will be more than secure from any aggression since the entire country is surrounded by sympathetic Arab countries as well as the presence of both Russia and the United States. An adequate police force coupled with whatever type militia or popular defense forces deemed practical by the Palestinian leaders would prove sufficient for civil order. Any continued insistence for an army, fully capable of waging conventional warfare would be highly suspect by all world leaders and governments. If efforts to achieve a lasting and just settlement have progressed to this point, it is doubtful the Israeli state would attack the Palestinian state without recognizing such an act could instigate a major conflict of worldwide proportions.

Thus far in our consideration of prerequisites to peace we have examined those elements I consider essential on the part of both the Israeli and Palestinian leadership. Admittedly, implementation of any one of these points will prove difficult and require real dedication by both principles. Difficult, but entirely possible!

THE PALESTINIAN STATE

An independent Palestinian State with true autonomy is a thinkable possibility for both Israeli and Arab citizens. To achieve this goal, several methods of bringing such a state about can be discussed.

(1) "Greater Jordan Concept"...basically, the occupied West Bank and Gaza Strip would revert back to a similar structure as was present prior to the 1967 invasion. At that time, Jordan occupied and administered the Old Jerusalem section of Palestine. Allowing this area to come under Jordanian oversight until a fully operational Palestinian State, with duly elected Palestinian leaders and government by and for the Palestinian inhabitants could be formed, would create the necessary safeguards to both Israeli and Palestinian, enabling the new State to be established and the existing Israeli State remaining unthreatened by the Arab State.

(2) United Nations Buffer Troops...a second possible method which has been succesfully used in the Sinai withdrawal as well as other "buffer" zones between southern Lebanon and northern Israel. U.N. troops could be stationed in a complete circle around the new Palestinian State between the Israeli boundaries and the new state. Obviously such a maneuver would require implicit trust by both parties, and absolute impartiality on behalf of all U.N. troops and their respective countries. If the Israeli leaders decry such a proposition, insisting they cannot entrust the security of their state to any foreign troops, the world will recognize the hyprocrisy of leaders who accept these same "peacekeeping" troops in other negotiated areas of the country but reject

them out of hand on the basis of intransigence and an unwillingness to obtain a lasting peace based upon true reparations.

If the returning Palestinian Arabs do not have a "standing army," there can be no validity to the Israeli accusation they must maintain military presence in order to protect their borders. One must expect an attitude of suspicion and distrust by both principals, but this must not be permitted to be used as an excuse for not attempting to establish a real peace through the establishment of an autonomous Palestinian State.

SUPPORTING ARAB STATES

For any negotiated settlement to take hold, it will be necessary for the various Arab countries to demonstrate their sincere desire for a just settlement to be concluded between the Palestinians and their Israeli counterparts. Some of the primary actions they must take include:

(1) Encourage and support the PLO/Palestinians to seek their own terms for peace with Israel. Surrounding states must remove themselves from the forefront of negotiations and allow only the Palestinian people to speak for themselves. This will require absolute political honesty in that none but the Palestinians can speak of their own needs and at what extent they will feel they have been fully compensated. Jordan would become involved only if and when requested by the Palestinian leadership. Syria would take up its own problems and differences with Israel on its own initiative, and not promote "linkage" which includes their own grievances along with the Palestinian situation. Likewise, Egypt would continue to forge its own future and destiny by speaking only for Egypt and its own relations with the Israeli state.

(2) Sign legal documents indicating their complete support for any accepted peace plan or proposals acceptable to the Palestinian people. Such a document would go far in assuring Israel and the world community that any true efforts expended to gain an equitable peace would not be sabotaged by any other Arab nation or people.

The formal documents could be composed from within the

United Nations body along with a public signing ceremony by all involved parties. The remaining U.N. members would affix their own signatures to the document as witnesses, thereby lending some assurance to the Israeli state that they would indeed be dealing with the Palestinian people alone.

(3) All supporting Arab countries would cease any and all acts of hostility, war, or aggression against the Israeli state to demonstrate their genuine concern for an immediate resolve of the issue. Such an act would demonstrate the united Arab desire for peace between Israel and the Palestinian people. Such cessation would also open the door for continued discussions and negotiations between aggrieved countries and Israeli leaders if such discussions were desired by both parties.

THE UNITED STATES MUST CHANGE ITS ATTITUDE

(1) The U.S. must openly demonstrate a true desire for a just and lasting peace between the two antagonists. American credibility will be slow in coming from among the world community because of the one-sided support of Israel maintained by the Congress. Politicians will have to sacrifice "voter appeal" for peace and stability. This will prove near impossible for some of the more "professional" politicians who have justified their election to the Congress on the basis of defending "little Israel" against any and all opposition, including justice and truth! The American people will have to DEMAND their elected representatives carry out the very act they are supposedly elected to do, namely, represent the wishes of their constituents with regard to a final settlement of the Middle East conflict. Unless the American people demand such action, it will not occur if left to the politicians who respond to lobby pressure and promises, rather than the good will and wishes of their constituency. If the United States is to be believed in desiring a truly just settlement, it must first demonstrate an even-handed attitude towards the Arab countries and more especially, the Palestinian people. Congressional leaders must not fear to speak openly of recognition of the PLO as the sole representative of the displaced Palestinians, nor be reluctant to advocate open dialogue with the PLO

and the United States. If both houses of Congress can be united in these efforts, then and only then can the President and the Executive branch be openly expected to lead the way in formulation of a new, even-handed policy towards the Palestinian issue. Admittedly, many citizens of the world community as well as those of the U.S. are quite skeptical as to the possibility of such a change in attitude and policy occurring, given the political prostitution conducted by many government leaders and lackeys. But a new awareness of the history and realities of the protracted conflict by America and its people can still produce political change. To this end this present work is dedicated.

(2) The United States must place the necessary pressure upon the Israeli leadership to settle the issue once and for all! The Zionist leadership will never, on its own resolve, initiate a just dialogue for ending hostilities as long as the immense Jewish Lobby of America assures them their every move and action will be supported and condoned by the "pocket politicians" in Washington. Like a schoolyard bully who stands a mere four feet in height yet challenges the entire student body simply because he knows "big brother" stands behind him and his rhetoric, the Begins, Sharons and Shamirs will cease their taunts and antagonistic acts only when learning their "big brother" no longer stands behind them and they alone are responsible for their actions and the ultimate outcome of those self-same actions. Naturally, there will be a great outcry of pain and accusation at any new change in attitude and policy, but change is always accompanied by dissent, and true growth accompanied by pain. If and until such pressure is applied by the U.S., the Israeli state will see little need of negotiations or pursuit of peace with its Arab neighbors.

(3) The United States must lead the way in suggesting a "buffer zone" between the borders of both "states," the current Israeli state and a new Palestinian state. The stationing of American troops between both would give an attempted settlement the necessary opportunity to work. Of course, the active participation by the U.S. in any final settlement must occur at the request and acceptance of both the Israelis and the Palestinians.

CHRISTIANS/CHURCHES MUST:

(1) Re-evaluate their "accepted" and/or "traditional" interpretations of biblical prophecy which have always been misconstrued as "pro-Zionist" and "pro-Israel." As we have seen in our study of Chapter 5, Zionism and the current state of Israel established in 1948 bear absolutely no relationship to the biblical Israel and the Abrahamic Covenant and promises given and CARRIED OUT in ancient history.

(2) Cease indiscriminate support of the Israeli state. God demands that governments act justly, uphold His standards, walk humbly before Him, and recognize His sovereignty. Some of the fiercest denunciations of social injustice, corruption, and immorality come from the Old Testament prophets like Amos, Micah and Jeremiah. The prophets all spoke boldly against the evils of their day and time, especially when the guilty party was their own government. God, the Scripture teaches, is not a respector of any individual or nation. The mere singing of "God Bless America" does not assure America of God's blessings or favor, just as the slogan "in God we trust" most certainly is not reflective of the collective attitude of American citizens. One has only to recall the bold denunciations of Isaiah, Joel, Hosea and the rest in order to understand that God has no "nation" or "peculiar people" apart from any and all who love and obey Him, and who include Him in their daily lives and living.

(3) Cease confusing political ideas with Scriptural teaching. Zionism is a HUMAN IDEOLOGY that many aethist Jews adhere to, totally devoid of any scriptural significance whatsoever! God is not bound by the puny theological charts and speculations of men, for history lies in His hands, not ours. He may choose to use the present Israeli state along with all other governments to fashion world policies and structure, but HE DOES NOT HAVE TO USE ISRAEL OR ANY OTHER NATION SIMPLY BECAUSE MEN SAY HE MUST! Perhaps the most flagrant juxtaposition of politics and scripture was evidenced by the recent bombing of the nuclear reactor in Iraq by the Israeli government. It was reported that same evening on the NBC network evening news program by

John Chancellor that Begin first contacted Mr. Jerry Falwell, leader of the "Moral Majority," asking Falwell to issue a statement to the press of Israel, stating that all American Christians were in total support of Israel's hostile act, and that such "activity" was actually "fulfilling prophecy" and therefore, God-sanctioned!

Despite the fact that no one can recall a worldwide election in which all Christendom elected Mr. Falwell absolute potentate and spokesman, he nonetheless issued a propaganda statement as requested by Menachem Begin. In an article in the Washington Star entitled "Begin Calls Falwell, Get Backing On Iraq" Falwell is quoted as saying.

"Mr. Prime Minister, I want to congratulate you for a mission that made us very proud that we manufacture those F-16s."

In an interview with Mr. John Rees in "The Review of the News, May 6, 1981, Falwell is quoted as saying on page 45:

"I doubt there is an organization in America that is so committed to the Jewish people everywhere and to the State of Israel. IN FACT, YOU CANNOT BELONG TO MORAL MAJORITY WITHOUT COMMITTING YOURSELF TO THE WELFARE OF THE STATE OF ISRAEL AND TO THE WELFARE OF THE JEWISH PEOPLE."
(Capital letters are mine, used for emphasis.)

One can only remain incredulous that Mr. Begin would request such an "approval" from Falwell, and that Falwell would presume to represent both God and Christianity in giving him such an answer! It is just such an attitude that has convinced the Arab people that American Christians are in total support of their extermination by the Israeli state.

Analyze the statements above. Moral Majority committed to truth? Committed to justice, and an equitable settlement of the Middle East conflict? No, rather committed to a political state and its policies. The Christian message must not be clouded by political favoritism and prejudice. The Middle East people remember the crusaders sent by the "church" who killed innocent people and ravaged their countries; they are aware that history records how the "church" appears a champion of colonial imperialism in Africa.

Is history now to record "church" endorsement of continued terror and aggression against an innocent people and their nation? Will it record the silence of America's spiritual leaders along with the masses who permit themselves to be intimidated and cajoled into shameful acquiescence for sake of popularity and acceptance among their peers?

A second "spokesman" lending considerable support to Begin and the Israeli state is Pat Robertson, founder of the Christian Broadcasting Network (CBN) and host of the "700 Club." Not only does Robertson openly support and favor Israel, but guests on his show endorse his personal views with religious justification and zeal. Here are just a few examples:

On July 28, 1981, the 700 Club featured Jay Rawlings, producer of a film "Apples of Gold," and clips from that film. The film purports to be a documentary on the history of Zionism and the founding of modern Israel. Rawling said:

> *"We Christians know in our hearts that God is on the side of Israel, not the terrorists. That is why we are trying to do what we can for Israel."*

Washington Post Journalist William Clairborne described "Apples of Gold" as "unabashedly one-sided, making no attempt to present the Palestinian viewpoint." (Washington Post, March 23, 1981, pg. A 11)

On April 26, 1982, the 700 Club guest was Mike Evans, author of *Israel, America's Key to Survival.* Evans claimed that the economic life of his home state of Alabama "miraculously" improved following letters of support sent to Israel by the state legislature.

On May 19, 1982, the 700 Club featured a special program "Israel: The Key to U.S. Security." The same scenario of Arab nations becoming communists and allying themselves with the Soviet Union was presented, with the prophecies from Ezekiel foretelling these events.

In a letter from Robertson to CBN Friends, April, 1982, pg. 1:

> *"I swore a vow to the Lord that despite the opposition to Israel on many sides, we would stand with Israel, come what may. And that was the turning point for the entire CBN ministry."*

The views and positions advocated by Falwell and Robertson along with many other "leaders" have done much to shape a large segment of conservative evangelicals into ardent supporters of the Israeli state. Consequently, the Palestinian people and the Arab nations in general are not viewed as a nation or entity, but mere pawns in a divine chess game of human history. They are untrustworthy, bloodthirsty demons of the underworld, and the enemies of God and "His people." Their resistance to the takeover of their country by Zionist militarism is seen as bold defiance of Almighty God! The sweeping identification of all Arabs with communism fuels the anti-Arab mentality just as surely as anti-Semitism against the Jews was fueled by calling them "Christ-killers" during World Wars I and II. Contempt for Arabs is intensified because they are the "enemies of Israel," and therefore, enemies of God as well!

Let it be stated that there is no basis for Christian opposition to the Arab people and the Palestinians in particular on the basis of Biblical teaching. Christians must cease allowing such misrepresentation by refusing to be a part of any of the polluted political ministries.

"OTHER VOICES" FROM THE STATE OF ISRAEL

Although the majority of Zionist citizens in Israel seem to support continued expansionism and settlement policies now being aggressively pursued by the current government, there are now, and have always been, a blend of voices, Israeli voices, decrying the continued acts of injustice and deceit. Such Israeli citizens have continued to oppose all annexation projects, correctly pointing out that such activities tend to merely exacerbate the Palestinian issue. Such men and women fear the results of present policies such as territorial expansion will bring neither peace nor security. They are not a majority, but their number are growing and their combined voices could make a considerable difference in the immediate future. In a recent issue of the New Orleans newspaper The Times-Picayne dated April 30, 1982, the account of several prominent Israeli citizens is recorded concerning the current occupation of Palestine and the displacement of its original inhabitants. Mr. Yehuda Elkana survived the gas chambers of Auschwitz, immigrated to Israel in 1948 and today is director of the prestigious Van Leer Institute in Jerusalem and professor of history and philosophy of science at Tel Aviv University.

"I still believe the moral issue is paramount. I don't think that any nation can keep its moral spirit, its self-respect for long ruling a million people against their wish under occupation. It just can't be done.

It is somewhat encouraging to note that not all Jews or Israelis have become mesmerized by the temporary political and military "power" of the Zionist state while ignoring the fact that the Jews survived through the centuries of history not by such power of their own, but the power of a just God seeking to implement moral truth in world society.

Mr. Elkana has chosen to articulate the crucial fact that any nation, state, or people who wage an ongoing war of oppression and injustice in an occupied land will, sooner or later, experience moral self-destruction. Mr. Elkana continues:

"So much energy goes into keeping up the occupation. There are simply not enough people to do the right thing for the country, which has to be developed. Then there are the sheer political terms. I am not a romantic about Arabs. I am not a romantic about Arafat. But the only chance we have is if we try them: if we accept the reality of Palestinian nationalism and they mutually accept ours. It is a risk, but not doing it is an infinitely bigger risk. We are heading toward turning 100 million Arabs into a terrorist army against us... the whole Arab world! The United States wants to support rational, moderate Arabs. And rational, moderate Arabs will tolerate Israel's occupation of Arab land less and less. So what is there to look forward to if we go on this way...?"

Thousands of Israeli citizens are now joining in the call for an end to the illegal seizure of lands, homes and businesses; an end to unlawful settlements upon land owned solely by the rightful Arab owners for untold centuries until taken over by European immigrants; an end to abrasive political actions designed solely for the purpose of agitation of their Palestinian neighbors and friends. Their voices are not strong, but they grow stronger! Will their own Israeli leaders listen? Will the world community listen? Are you listening to their voices? What will you do with their requests? What will you do with the knowledge you have gained from this book? Your attentiveness and action may well contribute to a final, lasting peace!

Security Council Resolution 242 for a Just and Lasting Peace

November 22, 1967

The Security Council,

Expressing its continuing concern with the grave situation in the Middle East,

Emphasizing further that all Member States in their acceptance of the Charter of the United Nations have undertaken a commitment to act in accordance with Article 2 of the Charter,

1. Affirms that the fulfillment of Charter principles requires the establishment of a just and lasting peace in the Middle East which should include the application of both the following principles:

   (i) Withdrawal of Israel armed forces from territories occupied in the recent conflict;

   (ii) Termination of all claims or states of belligerency and respect for and acknowledgement of the sovereignty, territorial integrity and political independence of every State in the area and their right to live in peace within secure and recognized boundaries free from threats or acts of force;

2. Affirms further the necessity

   (a) For guaranteeing freedom of navigation through international waterways in the area;

   (b) For achieving a just settlement of the refugee problem;

    (c) For guaranteeing the territorial inviability and political independence of every State in the area, through measures including the establishment of demilitarized zones;

3. Requests the Secretary-General to designate a Special Representative to proceed to the Middle East to establish and maintain contacts with the States concerned in order to promote agreement and assist efforts to achieve a peaceful and accepted settlement in accordance with the provisions and principles in this resolution;

4. Requests the Secretary-General to report to the Security Council on the progress of the efforts of the Special Representative as soon as possible.

"All that is necesssary for the forces of evil to win the world is for enough good men to do nothing."
Edmund Burke

BIBLIOGRAPHY

The Middle East and Palestine

Abu-Lughod, Ibrahim, ed. *The Transformation of Palestine.* Evanston: Northwestern University Press, 1971.

Alush, Naji. *Arab Resistance in Palestine, 1914-1948* (in Arabic). Beirut: Palestine Research Center, 1967.

Antonius, George. *The Arab Awakening.* Philadelphia: Lippincott, 1939.

Bell, J. Bowyer. *The Long War: Israel and the Arabs Since 1946.* Englewood Cliffs, N.J.: Prentice-Hall, 1969.

Dodd, Peter, and Halim Barakat. *River without Bridges: A Study of the Exodus of the 1967 Palestinian Refugees.* Beirut: Institute for Palestine Studies, 1968.

Furlonge, Sir Geoffrey. *Palestine is My Country: The Story of Musa Alami.* London: John Murray, 1969.

Hirst, David. *The Gun and the Olive Branch.* New York and London: Harcourt Brace Jovanovich, 1977.

Jeffries, J.M.N. *Palestine: The Reality.* London: Longmans, Green, 1939.

Khouri, Fred J. *The Arab-Israeli Dilemma.* Syracuse, N.Y.: Syracuse University Press, 1968.

Lillienthal, Alfred M. *The Zionist Connection.* New York: Dodd, Mead and Company, 1978.

Monroe, Elizabeth. *Britain's Moment in the Middle East.* Baltimore: Johns Hopkins Press, 1963.

Polk, William R., David H. Stamler, and Edmund Asfour. *Backdrop to Tragedy: The Struggle for Palestine.* Boston: Beacon Press, 1957.

Sharabi, Hisham. *Arab Intellectuals and the West: The Formative Years, 1875-1914.* Baltimore: Johns-Hopkins Press, 1970.

——. *Palestine and Israel: The Lethal Dilemma.* New York: Pegasus, 1969.

Toynbee, Arnold. "The McMahon-Hussein Correspondence: Comments and a Reply." Journal of Contemporary History, Vol. 5, No. 4, 1970.

Weizman, Ezer. *The Battle For Peace.* New York: Bantam Books, 1981.

Archaeological and Historical References

Albright, William F. *The Archaeology of Palestine.* Baltimore: Penguin Books, 1961.

Boyd, Robert. *Tells, Tombs, and Treasures.* Grand Rapids, Michigan: Baker, 1969.

Breasted, James H. *A History of Ancient Egypt.* New York: Charles Scribner's Sons, 1912.

Finegan, Jack. *Light From the Ancient Past.* New Jersey: Princeton University Press, 1946.

Free, Joseph P. *Archaeology and Bible History.* Wheaton, Illinois: Scripture Press, 1969.

Garstang, J. *The Story of Jericho.* London: Marshall, Morgan and Scott, 1948.

Gurney, O.R. *The Hittites.* Baltimore: Penguin Books, 1969.

Keller, Werner. *The Bible as History.* New York: Morrow, 1969.

Kenyon, Sir Fredrick. *The Bible and Archaeology.* New York: Harper and Brothers, 1949.

Kyle, Melvin G. *The Deciding Voice of the Monuments.* Oberlin, Ohio: Bibliotheca Sacra Co., 1924.

Marston, Charles. *New Bible Evidence.* New York: Revell, 1935.

Orr, James. *The International Standard Bible Encyclopedia, Vol. IV.* Grand Rapids, Michigan: Wm. B. Eerdmans, 1939.

Owen, Fredrick G. *Archaeology and the Bible.* New Jersey: Fleming H. Revell, 1961.

Petrie, Flinders. *Palestine and Israel.* London: Society for Promoting Christian Knowledge, 1934.

Pfeiffer, Charles F. and Howard F. Vos. *The Wycliffe Historical Geography of Bible Lands.* Chicago: Moody Press, 1967.

Pritchard, James B. *Archaeology and the Old Testament.* Princeton, New Jersey: Princeton University Press, 1958.

———. *The Ancient Near East Texts.* Princeton, New Jersey: Princeton University Press, 1958.

Schwantes, Siegfried J. *A Short History of the Ancient Near East.* Grand Rapids, Michigan: Baker Book House, 1965.

Schultz, Samuel J. *The Old Testament Speaks.* New York: Harper/Row, 1960.

Tenney, Merrill C. *Zondervan Pictorial Bible Dictionary.* Grand Rapids, Michigan: Zondervan, 1963.

Wooley, Leonard C. *Abraham——Recent Discoveries and Hebrew Origins.* New York: Charles Scribners Sons, 1936

Wright, Ernest G. *Biblical Archaeology.* Philadelphia: Westminster Press, 1957.

Hermeneutics and Biblical Interpretation

Dungan, Prof. D.R. *Hermeneutics, A Text-Book.* Arkansas: Gospel Light Publishing Company, 1900's.

Farrar, Fredric W. *History of Interpretation.* Grand Rapids, Michigan: Baker Book House, 1961.

Lockhart, Clinton. *Principles of Interpretation.* Kansas City: Central Seminary Press, 1952.

Stroop, Ridley J. *Why Do People Not See the Bible Alike?* Nashville, Tennessee: William Co., 1949.

Terrey, Milton S. *Biblical Hermeneutics.* Grand Rapids, Michigan: Zondervan Publishing House, n.d.

Biblical Prophecy

Allis, Oswald T. *Prophecy and the Church.* Philadelphia: Presbyterian and Reformed, 1945.

Bales, James D. *Prophecy and Premillennialism.* Searcy, 1972.

Brown, Francis, Driver, S.R., and Briggs, Chas A. *A Hebrew and English Lexicon of the Old Testament.* Oxford: Clarendon.

Butler, Paul T. *Daniel.* Joplin: College Press, 1970.

Cox, William E. *Biblical Studies in Final Things.* Philadelphia: Presbyterian and Reformed, 1967.

Crawford, C.C. *Genesis, Volumes I, II, III, IV.* Joplin: College Press, 1966-1971.

Davidson, A.B. *The Theology of the Old Testament.* (Ed. S.D.F. Salmond). Edinburgh: T. & T. Clark, 1904.

Davies, W.D., and Daube, D. (Eds.) *The Background of the New Testament and Its Eschatology.* Cambridge: University Press, 1956.

DeCaro, Louis A. *Israel Today: Fulfillment of Prophecy?* Philadelphia: Presbyterian and Reformed, 1974.

Delitzsch, Franz, "Isaiah" (Vol. I, II) Kiel & Delitzsch—Commentary on the Old Testament. Grand Rapids: Eerdmans, 1969.

Hendricksen, William E. *Israel in Prophecy.* Grand Rapids: Baker, 1974.

———. *More Than Conquerors.* Grand Rapids: Baker, 1940.

Hughes, Phillip E. *Interpreting Prophecy.* Grand Rapids: Eerdmans, 1976.

Jocz, Jakob, *"The Covenant: A Theology of Human Destiny"* Grand Rapids: Eerdmans, 1968.

Milton, John P. *Prophecy Interpreted.* Minneapolis: Augsburg, 1960.

Perry, Ray. *Christian Eschatology and Social Thought.* New York: Abingdon, 1956.

Thomas, Dr. Lewis. "Warts, Brains and Other Astonishments," Reader's Digest, pp. 97-100, October, 1979.

Walvoord, John F. *Israel in Prophecy.* Findlay: Dunham, 1974.

Wilson, Robert D. *Studies in the Book of Daniel.* Grand Rapids: Baker, 1979.

Young, Edward J. *The Prophecy of Daniel.* Grand Rapids: Eerdmans, 1980.

———. *The Book of Isaiah, Vol. I, II, III.* Grand Rapids: Eerdmans, 1965-1972.